In memory of Naomi Schor, friend and colleague

NUMBER 103

Yale French Studies

French and Francophone: The Challenge of Expanding Horizons

Yale French Studies

Farid Laroussi and Christopher L. Miller, *Special editors for this issue*

Alyson Waters, *Managing editor*

Editorial board: Edwin Duval (Chair), Joseph Acquisto, Ora Avni, R. Howard Bloch, Peter Brooks, Mark Burde, Brooke Donaldson, Shoshana Felman, Thomas Kavanagh, Christopher L. Miller, Donia Mounsef, Susan Weiner

Editorial assistant: Joseph Mai

Editorial office: 82-90 Wall Street, Room 308

Mailing address: P.O. Box 208251, New Haven, Connecticut 06520-8251

Sales and subscription office:
Yale University Press, P.O. Box 209040
New Haven, Connecticut 06520-9040
Published twice annually by Yale University Press

Designed by James J. Johnson and set in Trump Medieval Roman by The Composing Room of Michigan, Inc. Printed in the United States of America by the Vail-Ballou Press, Binghamton, N.Y.

ISSN 044-0078
ISBN for this issue 0-300-10015-9

FARID LAROUSSI AND
CHRISTOPHER L. MILLER

Editors' Preface:
French and Francophone:
The Challenge of Expanding Horizons

This volume of *Yale French Studies* analyzes the most significant change in the field of French studies since the theoretical and feminist revolutions of the 1970s: the rise of "Francophone" literatures within French departments and, consequently, the necessity of reappraising the discipline as a whole. For it was not merely an addition of new texts that took place in the 1980s and 1990s; it was the arrival of new points of view and new questions about the nature of literature and culture. Rather suddenly, the horizons expanded, and French studies became "multicultural," perhaps against its will. Starting from a neat hexagon with a relatively clear canon in the early to mid-twentieth century, then moving to a (still) neat hexagon with a deconstructed and partially feminized canon in the 1970s, scholars and students of French in the 1980s and 1990s found that the geographical and cultural basis of their field was being called into question. The purely temporal division of the discipline into subfields coterminous with the centuries (*dix-huitiémiste, vingtiémiste*, etc.) was now challenged by a spatial model. France, while still in a position of unquestioned dominance, was nonetheless one "area" of possible interest in a field that now included Sub-Saharan Africa, the Maghreb, Quebec, the Caribbean, and even Vietnam. (We have not attempted to account for the *francophonie* of European nations like Belgium and Switzerland, which are not former colonies of France and therefore not part of the same problematic.) France was not alone; its former colonies would now be heard within literary and academic discourse. But how would those two systems for institutionalizing literature—one temporal and one spatial—coexist?

This volume of *Yale French Studies* is concerned with the emergence of new relations between "French" and "Francophone" in institutions, in pedagogy, and in interpretations of literature and culture.

YFS 103, *French and Francophone*, ed. Farid Laroussi and Christopher L. Miller, © 2003 by Yale University.

Since the purpose of this entire enterprise is to examine shifting definitions of "French" and "Francophone" in the academy and beyond, we shall dispense with the quotation marks around those words.[1]

There was a considerable lag between the emergence of Francophone literatures in France's colonies (in most cases in the early twentieth century) and the acceptance of those literatures in academies around the world (a process that is documented in this volume). Until quite recently, Francophone African, Canadian, and Caribbean literatures were rare and marginalized in most American French departments; in the past decade or so, they have become far more accepted and enfranchised. Most departments offer at least one course in one of these fields, and in many departments Francophone literatures have had a considerable impact on the curriculum, on dissertation research, and on the terms of literary debate. But now that these materials are being taught, many questions remain: What does this new presence mean for French studies as a whole? On the practical level, with reduced enrollments in French, how can more (and more diverse) materials be covered with fewer resources? In terms of curriculum, should Francophone materials be "integrated" (or "assimilated") into a framework that remains the same, or do they require a more general restructuring of the system? What new demands are made on students as a result of the presence of Francophone literatures, in both undergraduate French majors and Ph.D. programs? Is French no longer a cohesive field? Or is a new, global "French and Francophone" field emerging, with a new coherence of its own? These questions of course run parallel to social issues in France itself and in France's relations to its former colonies and current *Départements d'Outre-Mer* and *Territoires d'Outre-Mer:* immigration, integration, nationalism, the attempt to form a sort of commonwealth under the aegis of *francophonie,* the rise of the European Union, and of course globalization. The core question in our inquiry here is thus: What has been, what is, and what should be the relation between metropolitan French literary studies and Francophone literatures from around the world?

The essays presented here originated in a conference that took place at Yale in November 1999.[2] Rather than a formal presentation of pa-

1. For an overview of this question see Francesca Canadé Sautman, "Hip–Hop/ scotch: Sounding Francophone in French and United States Cultures, *France/USA: The Culture Wars, Yale French Studies* 100 (2001): 119–45.
2. For an account of the conference, see Daniel Delas, "French and Francophone," *Études littéraires africaines* 8 (1999): 25–26.

pers, the conference was a forum for discussion of issues that had not yet been faced systematically: the implications of the arrival on the scene of Francophone literatures. According to those who were there, what made that conference so unique was the fact that it brought together—in one room rather than in separate panels at a colloquium—scholars from both "sides," French and Francophone, specifically to discuss and to question the configuration of the discipline. Numerous participants came away saying they simply had had no idea how things looked from the other point(s) of view.

This volume is made up of scholarly papers that grew out of, and which presumably were influenced by, those discussions. The first section addresses our subject in terms of time; the second in terms of space; the third is devoted to the broadest questions about French and Francophone Studies as a discipline. Contributors were given rather strict space limitations.

Part one, "Institutional and Professional Histories," documents the arrival of Francophone literatures in United States French departments, as told from a variety of perspectives. Each contributor to this section has been a participant in this process as well as an observer of it; each reflects here on the circumstances (administrative, cultural, political, and personal) in which non-metropolitan literatures entered French departments. Ronnie Scharfman writes as an alumna of the Yale French department and as a pioneer in Francophone studies; she describes what it was like to work on an author like Aimé Césaire before the categories of Francophone and postcolonial had been formalized to support such an inquiry. Réda Bensmaïa evokes the "clandestine" beginnings of Francophone pedagogy: how he (and others) slipped nonhexagonal literature into the program of French studies. He also meditates on the philosophical burden of alterity that has so often been associated with Francophone literatures. Karen Gould shows how the habitual American ignorance of Canada has been partially overcome in some French departments in the United States and how the politics of Quebec nationalism and feminism have played an important role in this process. Samba Gadjigo's historical overview of the arrival of African literature in United States French departments tells the story of a process of curricular expansion that is far from complete. His essay logically leads to the questions of how the problems of institutional exclusion and assimilation—evident in each of the essays in this first section—have been addressed abroad, in the Francophone world itself. That is the subject of our second section.

"Configurations of French and Francophone around the World" is a concise survey of our subject in France and the Francophone world. How have the notions of "French" and "Francophone" been constructed in these different spheres and nations? What are the institutional and intellectual relations between the metropolitan canon and Francophone literatures in these contexts? Daniel Delas shows to what extent the French system of higher education refuses to recognize Francophone literatures, and he reveals the institutional structure of that refusal. He underlines the difficulties posed by the thickets of cultural ideologies in a country where literature is coextensive with identity, and identity politics are considered dangerous. Jean Jonassaint's comparison of Haitian and French Caribbean (that is, Martinican and Guadeloupean) literatures accounts for the fundamental differences between these closely related cultural spheres. By bringing to the fore issues such as language (French, Creole languages) and shared history, Jonassaint's article speaks directly to those interested in Francophone Caribbean cultural identities. Amadou Koné evokes his professional experiences in Côte d'Ivoire, in France, and now in the United States, in order to raise questions about the teaching of African literature in different contexts. Josias Semujanga examines Quebecois literature within Canadian academe; he shows how, in order to form and defend its own canon, Quebec has resorted to a nationalistic discourse and limited the attention given to other Francophone literatures. By so doing, Semujanga explains how in fact Quebecois literature might possibly be the only Francophone literature that has found its own voice against both France's cultural dominance and the English language hegemony in North America. Farid Laroussi touches on the ambiguous position of the French language throughout the Maghreb. His essay discusses the role of the writer under social and political scrutiny in particular, as well as political reforms that have attempted (and failed) to reform the status of the "colonial" language.

In the third section, "Impact, Influence, and Interpretation," we asked scholars to take a broad view: either by discussing how interpretation has changed with the advent of Francophone literature or by demonstrating this change through examples of reading practice. Has the arrival of Francophone literatures altered the way we read all literature now in this discipline? The approaches taken in this section vary widely and exhibit a range of attitudes toward the centripetal and centrifugal forces that govern France and the Francophone world. The first two essays exemplify new approaches to the terms "French" and "Francophone": they show, implicitly, how those two terms are lived and represented in literature; the remaining three articles discuss the condition of French and Francophone studies explicitly. J. Michael Dash reads the travel writing of the French surrealists as "a new anthropological discourse" that made a mark on the Francophone Caribbean writing that followed; here the encounter between French and Francophone seems to transcend colonial binarism and evolve into forms of transnationalism. The note of "salutary" optimism on which Dash ends his essay stands in marked contrast to the situation described by Francesca Canadé Sautman in her analysis of African novels of the 1980s. Here the formlessness of postmodernism, the myth of the global village, and the agenda of a smooth *francophonie* that transcends borders are *not* helpful constructs but rather masks over violent hegemony; resistance takes the form of giving voice to the "unspeakable"— even in French. At the level of institutional programs, how can models as disparate as those proposed by Dash and Canadé Sautman be accommodated? Do Francophone literatures blend into the French curriculum? Mireille Rosello reflects with some bemusement on the inevitable institutional reification of a category like the Francophone, once it as been recognized: as a "happy yet recalcitrant Francophonist," she gently resists the movement toward the hardening of categories and specializations. As a safeguard against the possible balkanization of French and Francophone studies, Rosello calls for a continual process of "unhoming." The section closes with an implicit dialogue between two scholars of French literature (though neither read the other's text). Sandy Petrey sounds a note of caution as he defends the idea of the center and of France as the necessary center of anything called French Studies. He asks how coherence can be maintained in a context of diminishing enrollments and reduced staff on the one hand, and an expanded, Francophone curriculum on the other. Petrey's strong defense of a centripetal model is then countered by Lawrence Kritzman's vision of an expanded and continually expanding field. In the deconstructive tradition he sees a way to move forward by teaching "students to think of the discipline of French otherwise." This group of five essays thus offers an overview of the tensions, ambiguities, and insights of French and Francophone studies at the beginning of the new century.

The preparation of this volume was marked by an event of great sadness to us and to the community of scholars in general: the untimely death of our colleague Naomi Schor. A vital participant in the conference from which this volume emerged, Naomi was slated to contribute to our third section. As a leader of the feminist reappraisal of the French canon in the 1970s and after, recently engaged in a new project on the problem of universalism in French culture that brought her into contact with Francophone authors like Senghor, Naomi was ideally suited to reflect on the arrival of Francophone literature. On the day before she was stricken by a cerebral hemorrhage, she handed over the text that we print here without alteration. The questions that she raises in these few pages are characteristically penetrating. This short essay stands as a testimony to her brilliance, allowing us to hear her voice again; its brevity is a sign of a career cut short.

In a generous act of mourning, Tom Conley then rewrote his own contribution to this volume, dedicating it to Naomi. His thesis is one to which we subscribe: that Naomi Schor's work, with its emphasis on the "alienating powers of literature," offers a new way forward, taking us beyond the binarism of French and Francophone as separate spheres. The "salutary truth," Conley writes, is that "all French literature is Francophone." This provides a fitting conclusion: even as we mourn the loss of Naomi, we can rededicate ourselves to the intellectual openness and rigor that she embodied; it is surely those qualities that can help us find a path toward the future of French—and Francophone—studies.

We wish to thank the Yale Department of French, the Cultural Service of the French Embassy, the Whitney Humanities Center, and the Kempf Fund for their support of the conference on which this volume is based. That event would not have been possible without the tireless efforts of Stephanie Reid. And we are grateful to Alyson Waters for her work on this volume.

I. Institutional and Professional Histories

RONNIE SCHARFMAN

Before the Postcolonial

" . . . do not make of me this man of hatred for whom I feel only
hatred. . . . "
—Aimé Césaire

"What is poetry which does not save nations and peoples?"
—Czelaw Milosz

This essay will explore, in a personal and historical narrative, the experience I had in my Yale Graduate School career as a fledgling Francophone specialist in a field that did not as yet exist. What was it like
to formulate a conceptual model for poetry that was, in the case of Aimé
Césaire on whom I wrote my doctoral dissertation and subsequent
book, both a discourse of the subject and an anticolonial engagement,
at a time when French theory—deconstruction in particular—was at
its height in American departments of French? In what ways did the benign marginalization to which I was subjected in making my choice of
thesis topic enact and prefigure tensions and resistances that still challenge the traditional hexagonal curriculum organized by century or
genre?

When I first came to the Yale French Department as a graduate student in 1971, I had two articles of baggage that were to have an endur-
ing impact on my course of study: the first-hand experience of the student uprisings in May 1968 in France, and the discovery there of the
work of the Martinican poet, Aimé Césaire. During the academic year
1967–68, I was a Fulbright scholar in Aix-en-Provence, working on a
Licence-ès-Lettres in Surrealism with Professor Antoine Raybaud. It
was in the context of this course that I was first introduced to the poetry of Césaire and, despite the lexical difficulties of his text, I imme-

YFS 103, *French and Francophone,* ed. Farid Laroussi and Christopher L. Miller,
© 2003 by Yale University.

diately felt compelled by what André Breton characterized as the "unceasingly major quality of the tone" that defines great poetry.[1]

The poet's struggle, as colonized subject, to constitute a disalienated identity in poetry, to forge a French language capable of expressing what Césaire calls his "*moi-nègre,*" his use of the poetic image, that surrealist royal road to the unconscious, and of rhythms called up from his deepest self, all of this was tremendously appealing to me as an outsider to everything about France and the French language that I was attempting to master, and that would become the focus of my commitment as a professor. The painful honesty of Césaire's struggle, which consisted not only in a violent denunciation of the scandal of colonialism, but also in an identity quest that required acknowledging the shame of slavery and confronting the racist stereotypes that were its sequellae—all these created a text that seemed to me of the utmost power and urgency. And the humanistic utopianism of Césaire's prayer to his heart in the *Notebook of a Return to the Native Land,* "what I want / is for universal hunger / for universal thirst," was particularly apt for those of us lifted up on the idealistic wave of the student movement of May '68.[2] At the same time, all of Césaire's work as a poet, essayist, playwright, and political leader, from the publication of the *Notebook* in 1939 on, challenged from the margins the authority, institutions, and ideology of the French metropolitan center in an effort to decolonize the mind. This would lay the groundwork for postcolonial studies. His work resonated with the goals of the Civil Rights struggle and the anti-Vietnam War movement that had characterized my college years.

At Yale in the early '70s, the French Department was offering standard courses on canonical authors and themes, but also introducing students to French theory as "instruments and methods," a course on tools for critical analysis taught jointly by Shoshana Felman and Jean Gaudon. Paul de Man was teaching classes on Rousseau, Mallarmé, Proust; Georges May on Diderot; Victor Brombert on Flaubert and the Symbolist Poets; Shoshana Felman on Modernity, Repetition in Literature; Peter Brooks on Melodrama; Jacques Guicharnaud on Contemporary French Theater; Imbry Buffum on Montaigne.

There was nothing that remotely resembled a course on non-Hexag-

---

1. André Breton, "Un grand poète noir," preface to Aimé Césaire, *Cahier d'un retour au pays natal* (Paris: Présence africaine, third edition, 1971).
2. Césaire, *Cahier d'un retour au pays natal.*

onal or postcolonial Francophone literature. The corpus and its relationship not only to metropolitan France, but also to the traditional
curriculum, the very notion that the "Empire" could write back, had
simply not been defined. Then, in my second year, a junior faculty
member from Anglophone Africa, Hilary Okam, taught a thematically
organized seminar on Aimé Césaire. By the time professor Okam edited
what I would consider the first approach of *Yale French Studies* to part
of the Francophone corpus—a volume on "Traditional and Contemporary African Literature" in 1976—he had already left Yale for York College, CUNY. Another junior faculty member in the department,
George Joseph, had spent several years in Senegal and was an enthusiastic reader of its Francophone literature. We would compare reading
notes in the corridors of William L. Harkness Hall, forming our own secret society.

In terms of literary theory, we were reading Derrida and Lacan,
Barthes and Foucault and Kristeva. Authors were dead, writing was in-
transitive, subjectivity was decentered, fragmented, alienated, history
did not exist, there was no referent. There were only texts, whose play
of signifiers was always suspect and susceptible to deconstruction. Indeed, it was incumbent upon us in certain classes to perform deconstructive readings of the text, lest we fall into the literary limbo of the
hermeneutic error.

Given the intellectual climate of the Yale French Department at the
time and the lack of mentors and reading strategies for approaching
postcolonial texts, it was a real challenge for me to formulate a theoretical framework that would allow me to articulate what would best
capture the complex relationship in Césaire's poetry between a colonized, black subject struggling to constitute itself in the language Sartre
had designated as the "enemy's thinking apparatus," and some discourse of anticolonial engagement. Except for that one Césaire seminar, no courses addressed any of these issues either in theory or in content. The postcolonial did not yet exist, and the analytic categories of
which young Francophone scholars can now avail themselves had not
yet been thought.

My own readings in what are considered the founding texts of the
colonial dialectic, especially Frantz Fanon's *Black Skin, White Masks*
and *The Wretched of the Earth*, Sartre's "Orphée noir," and Albert
Memmi's *Portrait of the Colonized*, helped me to theorize the model
that would be the undergirding for my thesis: the relationships of alterity as they function in the poetic text, the poetic subject positing it-

self against the other as a form of resistance to erasure, both personal and collective, and the forging of a new language in which to constitute itself as disalienated. Although there was nobody in the department to provide any guiding expertise, it did totally encourage free inquiry, and I will always be grateful that Paul de Man agreed to be my thesis advisor with the understanding between us that I would be working completely on my own. My marginalization within the department, what I perceived at times as benign indifference and at others as incredulity or even disdain, was therefore both inevitable, given the academic currents of the time and the faculty in the department, and of my own choosing. Unconsciously identified, then, with the poet I was seeking to elucidate, I devised a problematic which, it strikes me in retrospect, was not unlike the reading I gave, in the dissertation-turned-book, of Césaire's "coming-to-the-term-Negritude":

> . . . the poetic subject transforms the nostalgic mode into the creative one, establishing negritude at the forefront of the opposition. The battle begins with a new signifier, constituted from past values combined with rules from the language of the other . . . the word itself stands as a figure for the very forcing of the limits of possibility that characterizes the *Cahier*. At once primitive and poetic, African and ur-French, it combines what it needs from the ancestral past and from the poetic past to forge a new identity for the subject. The subject has found a model that can reconcile its poetic ambition, its intellectual engagement vis-à-vis the other 'horribles travailleurs' of poetry, and its visceral engagement vis-à-vis the people.[3]

Instinctively gravitating toward analyses that had been elaborated from the position of the colonized, I was able to avoid to some extent what would come to be critiqued among certain postcolonial critics as the extension of colonialist relations of power by those who utilized only Eurocentric theoretical tools to interpret Third World texts. That Memmi was steeped in Sartre, Fanon in Freud, and Césaire in Marx and the entire Western philosophical traditions only added to their arsenal of "miraculous weapons." Discovering these texts by colonized Francophone writers from the Antilles and the Maghreb was the condition of possibility of my thinking the first and most theoretical chapter of my dissertation, which I entitled "Critical Models of Engagement." In that chapter, I elaborated the notion of "engagement" as Sartre had the-

---

3. Ronnie Leah Scharfman, *Engagement and the Language of the Subject in the Poetry of Aimé Césaire* (Gainesville, Florida: University of Florida Press, 1987), 64.

orized it, and it comes close to what Helen Tiffin, some twenty years later, would analyze as "Counter Discourse." The rest of the thesis makes use of this apparatus in conjunction with close readings of Césaire's poetry.

It is here, I think, that the unique training in reading literary texts I received at Yale from professors like Paul de Man and Shoshana Felman provided me with invaluable tools. Deconstruction and psychoanalysis, as instruments for a practice of reading, allowed me to lay bare the deep tragic and ironic dimensions of Césaire's text, as well as its contestatory violence and its utopian politics. To this day I consider it a compliment that one of the readers of my Césaire manuscript, after it had been awarded a Gilbert Chinard literary prize and was being considered for publication by the University of Florida Press, snidely commented in his evaluation that "Scharfman is still under the sway of her Yale gurus."

What, then, were these critical models of the colonial dialectic that I was able to identify through my readings of these founding essays? I don't think it can be stressed enough that Memmi's *Portrait du Colonisé*, published in 1957, provided an invaluable analytical tool for apprehending the decolonization movements in the post-World-War-II Maghreb and Sub-Saharan Africa, as well as the literature denouncing colonization being produced in the '50s and '60s throughout much of the Francophone world, such as Césaire's *Discours sur le colonialisme*, of 1955.[4] The field of postcolonial studies has accustomed us today to think of much of the cultural production from emerging nations and immigrant populations in Western countries from the point of view of situation, rather than of identity. The concepts of hybridity, métissage, multiculturalism, bilingualism, migrations, all speak to the fluid and multiple ways postcolonial peoples describe themselves. The flexibility and relativity of boundaries that characterize contemporary cultural border work were not, however, operative in the colonized countries of the Francophone world in the 1950s. The struggle at the time, for writers like Memmi, Fanon, and Césaire, was to construct an identity in the face of the erasure of the history of the colonized, and in the face of the reification of the colonized other that Europe had effected in

---

4. Albert Memmi, *Portrait du colonisé, précédé du portrait du colonisateur* (Paris: Corré, 1957; English translation: *The Colonizer and the Colonized*, trans. Howard Greenfield (Boston: Beacon Press, 1991); Césaire, *Discours sur le colonialisme* (Paris: Présence africaine, 1955); English translation: *Discourse on Colonialism*, trans. Joan Pinkham (New York: Monthly Review Press, 2000).

order to justify its imperialist project of colonial exploitation, which included, at its origins, the scandalous oppression of slavery.

Memmi's sober portrait of the colonized identifies the formation of such a creature, the offenses committed against him, his slow awakening to anger and revolt, and the possible alternatives for action open to him. His analysis of the language of reification of the other employed systematically by the colonizer, with its dehumanizing and depersonalizing negations and pluralization, its accusation of racial inferiority, laid bare an ideological form of aggression universally operative in the colonial situation. The imposition of the French language is analyzed as denying the colonial subject the very capacity to constitute itself as such, thereby impeding its appropriation of history or its projection of self into the future.

Within the context of this analysis, I was able to read Césaire's poetry as an alienated subject's attempt to reinstate and reinsert itself as the subject of a previously occluded history. But what is missing in Memmi's analysis is the specificity of race relations and the specificity of the economic and geographical situation of the French Antilles. These I found in the work of the psychiatrist Frantz Fanon. A Martinican compatriot and one-time student of Césaire, Fanon deals with a community of problems that is strikingly similar, and Césaire's *Cahier* often voices the pain of what Fanon calls the "lived experience of the black man" in his psychoautobiography, *Peau noire, masques blancs*.[5] Like Césaire, Fanon as writing subject is striving toward the universal, but is forced back onto an exploration of the specificity of his black identity by the accusing, humiliating gaze of the white colonialist through whom he discovers his "being-for-others." Caught in what he himself acknowledges as a kind of double bind of the Sartrian relations of otherness, Fanon experiences a psychological and philosophical impasse. The ensuing rage and despair opens for Fanon onto the commitment to revolution.

Although Césaire chose to fight by remaining at home, as it were, entering a political career after World War II that he only now, at age 89, has given up completely, his poetry parallels Fanon's evolution as a political thinker. It is not within the scope of this essay to rehearse the conception and reception of Césaire's neologism "Negritude." Suffice it to say that it has been much critiqued by both Third World writers

5. Frantz Fanon, *Peau noire, masques blancs* (Paris: Éditions du Seuil, 1952); English translation: *Black Skin, White Masks*, trans. Charles Lamb Markmann (New York: Grove Press, 1982).

and postcolonial critics as everything from essentialist and Afrocentric to reversely racist, all of which have been deeply wounding to Césaire. At the time I wrote my dissertation, however, I argued that the coming-to-the-term, that the coming to terms with an Afro-Caribbean identity for the young Césaire writing in the late 1930s had necessarily to pass through an identification with Africa, with its cultural values, but also with the history of slavery. This is the function of negritude in the *Cahier*. With hindsight, it is tempting to grant Sartre a certain degree of prescience in his prediction that negritude, as the weak moment in the colonial dialectic, was destined to be transcended and to disappear. Certainly in the French Antilles, with Glissant's concept of "*antillanité*," positing a common identity for Caribbeans based first of all on geography and the history of plantation culture, and Bernabé, Chamoiseau, and Confiant's concept of "*créolité*" as constructing an identity based on linguistic and anthropological commonalities that stress the hybrid nature of creoleness, we find combinations and permutations of some of the identity questions posed by Césaire and Fanon, minus the racial component. Even Fanon, arguing later in his revolutionary *Les damnés de la terre*, came to characterize that very Césairian Negritude that had permitted him to describe the alienated situation of the black colonized subject as irresponsible because, he explains, it regressively revalorizes the past, on the one hand, and, on the other, in its appeal to all people of color it threatens the thrust for national liberation.[6]

Fanon's analysis of the stages of evolution of the colonized writer in the move toward a revolutionary consciousness proved also to be an invaluable tool for formulating my problematic. Specifically, it helped me understand the tragic aspects of Césaire's effort to move from the individual to the collective, from poetry to action. Reading Fanon with Césaire, then, allowed me to gauge and delineate certain critical differences, to devise the notion of "islandness" as a figure for poetic form, for self-imposed structure from within which the poet poses certain questions in and of language, as well as a figure for rootedness and the decision to stay in Martinique and forge a disalienated consciousness from within.

My dissertation was, thankfully, enthusiastically received by my advisor and my committee of readers, for whom I have reason to believe

---

6. Fanon, *Les damnés de la terre* (Paris: François Maspero, 1961); English translation: *The Wretched of the Earth*, trans. Constance Farrington (New York: Grove Press, 1982).

it was something of an eye-opener. Nobody, however, had any ideas for me as to what to do with it. Moreover, when I was formulating my thesis topic, nobody had advised me about the difficulties of getting a monograph published. When I sent it to Professor Léon-François Hoffmann at Princeton, an early specialist in Francophone Haitian literature who had generously offered to read it, he suggested that I publish it as articles. Having taken so long to write it, I knew that it had to be my first book, and therefore held out to publish it in its entirety. This proved to be difficult, since not only was it a monograph, but also, in 1979, Césaire was still relatively unknown in the United States, and I had no mentor at Yale who would go to bat for me. Only through the serendipity of its winning a prize did it find a publisher.

At the MLA in 1983, I participated on a panel entitled, "Teaching Francophone Literature." I believe it was the first ever, and it was a somewhat naïve "report from the trenches" examining, in one case, the difficulty of having any such literature accepted at all in the French department curriculum. My own paper investigated the Eriksonian model of the adolescent identity crisis as a theme in Maghreb and Caribbean Francophone texts in an effort to make this corpus seem more "relevant." We were still striving for legitimacy.

The field of Postcolonial Francophone Studies has grown enormously since the late 1970s. We have wonderful theoretical tools to work with now, including those of Homi Bhabha, Chris Bongie, Édouard Glissant, Françoise Lionnet, Christopher Miller, Mireille Rosello, Edward Said, Helen Tiffen, and others. The literary corpus, too, keeps growing, and that, despite the pessimistic predictions of Memmi and Fanon, who prophesied the demise of French as a language of writing once independence became a reality for the (ex)colonies. French remains a lingua franca for many of those who, like the Moroccan Francophone writer Abdelkebir Khatibi, considers himself a "colonized-decolonized intellectual." And the issue in the academy is no longer "if," but rather "how" to integrate both the literature and the theory into our courses, as this volume of *Yale French Studies* attests.

While Yale felt in some ways like a desert for me as I wrote my dissertation, I was granted total intellectual freedom. It is both gratifying and exciting to me to see the growth of this field within the French Department, and I like to think I helped pave the way, institutionally, for other "horribles travailleurs" who came after.

RÉDA BENSMAÏA

~~Francophonie~~

> "Being is relation": but Relation is safe from the idea of Being . . .
> That which would preexist (Relation) is vacuity of Being-As-Being . . .
> Relation does not assert Being, except to distract.
> —Édouard Glissant, "That Those Beings
> Be Not Being," *Poetics of Relation*[1]

In a text he wrote on the occasion of the 1989 "États Généraux de la Francophonie," Abdelkebir Khatibi commented:

> For some time, we have already stopped speaking of "French literature," and we speak instead of "Francophone literatures." [To do so] assumes that there is indeed a *plurality*, a *diversity of literary languages*, and that this plurality is active; for without works created in the heart of *each of these languages, there would be no true international and intercultural experience.* . . . One is *[therefore] entitled to ask*. . . . : *is this designation ("Francophone literatures") a mere statement of fact, or does it refer to an entirely new and essential situation,* one that *brings into play* not only French literature, but in a radical (in the sense of roots and a diversity of roots) way, the French language *as a principle of identity?*[2]

I recall Khatibi's remarks here because they seem to me wholly relevant to the questions we were asked for this volume of *Yale French*

---

1. Édouard Glissant, "That Those Beings Be Not Being," in *Poetics of Relation*, trans. Betsy Wing (Ann Arbor: University of Michigan Press, 1997), 185–86.

2. Patrick Chamoiseau explains this question in terms of the Caribbean writer, but the "existential" situation he describes is the same for anyone who lives in a "dominated country": "How can you write when your imagination nourishes itself, from morning till dreaming, with images, thoughts, values that are not yours? How can you write when you vegetate outside of the impetuses that determine your life?" Patrick Chamoiseau, *Ecrire en pays dominé* (Paris: NRF, Gallimard, 1997), 17.

YFS 103, *French and Francophone*, ed. Farid Laroussi and Christopher L. Miller, © 2003 by Yale University.

17

Studies regarding our relationship to *Francophonie,* how things had begun for us here in the United States, the nature of the "reception" of
our course proposals, the obstacles put in our path, the encouragements
we were given, and so on.

When I got my first teaching position in the United States in 1981
at the University of Minnesota, to be recruited by a *French* department
meant something very precise: we were to have thoroughly studied the
history of *French* literature and to have worked on writers and subjects
that had primarily turned us into "specialists" of a "century" or a "period" in the history of this literature.

At the time and in these circumstances, there could obviously be no
question of challenging the nature of or the justification for the literature and language we were to teach. To be recruited by a French department in the 1980s meant that we were to teach purely French writers [*des écrivains franco-français*] who belonged to a purely French
literature, to students who were primarily interested in purely French
writers, in a language itself supposed to be purely French. For my part,
I can say (pastiching Jacques Derrida) that at the time, as a teacher of
literature written *in the French language:* 1) I could have only *one language,* and it wasn't mine and 2) I could teach only *one literature*
(French) and it wasn't mine either![3] That is, to be a teacher of French
(in a French department) in the 1980s meant that one was automati-
cally a teacher of *French* literature. The syllabi of the courses I taught
in the French and Comparative Literature Departments at the University of Minnesota, and later at the University of Virginia, reveal that all
the courses I offered dealt with a purely *French* literary corpus. This
does not mean that it never occurred to me to propose other courses or
to explore other literary horizons. There was just no demand for them.

When I began teaching in the United States, I had already published
a good number of articles on authors who did not belong to the purely
French sphere, writers as different from one another as Kateb Yacine,
Assia Djebar, Nabile Farès, Mouloud Feraoun, and Abdelkebir Khatibi.
Yet it was as if this literature belonged to an entirely different intellectual order, another "era" even of thought and culture. Granted, these
articles of mine had been published in *France* in specialized journals
that did not reach a broad public—the readership was made up almost
entirely of literary historians. Still, publications or no publications, I

3. Jacques Derrida, *Monolingualism of the Other, or the Prosthesis of Origin,* trans.
Patrick Mensah (Stanford, CA: Stanford University Press, 1998).

was never asked to design or teach any classes directly and primarily related to Francophone writers before I came to Brown. No one had ever thought of asking me to do so.

As I would better understand with time, the real reason for this veritable "black out" when it came to Francophone literature was simply that Francophone writers were not an integral part of the French literary *canon,* and so could not find their way into the American *curriculum.* This is why, for so long, any support I was given, whether moral or material, came from pioneers such as Jacqueline Arnauld, Jean Dejeux, and Charles Bonn in France, or from Francophone scholars in Canada. I published my first critical text on Maghrebi Francophone literature thanks to Arnauld, who was one of the few scholars and teachers of Francophone literature in France at the time. She was extremely attentive to young scholars who were interested in this literature and in what was happening outside the Hexagon.

Today I see clearly that what we now call "Francophone literature" had been, back then, and for each and every one of us, the object of a veritable *scotomization process,* a primordial interdict even: we knew that this literature existed, but we behaved *officially* as if it did not. I said that there was no "demand." But neither was there any administrative or pedagogical infrastructure supported by "political" decisions. In the 1970s and 1980s, there were almost no positions for the teaching of Francophone literature, and the conditions for its "inscription" in the university curriculum were lacking.

As Derrida showed so clearly in *The Monolingualism of the Other,* the "interdict" or "black out" I mentioned above was long-standing, stemming directly from a (colonial) educational system that left no room for the *differences* that put pressure on both the language and the literatures that came out of it. If it is true that the "monolingualism of the other" is "[f]irst and foremost . . . that sovereignty, that law originating from elsewhere . . . but also primarily the very language of the Law" (39) and if it is true that such a "sovereignty"—whose "essence is always colonial," as Derrida affirms, tends "repressively and irrepressibly to reduce language to the One, that is, to the hegemony of the homogeneous" (40), we can easily see how so-called "Francophone" literature was for so long the object of a scotomization. Inscribed *within us,* the "law" (of language) as a manifestation of the colonial power about which Derrida speaks did not need, in order to exercise its power (of de-negation), "to organize any spectacular initiatives: religious missions, philanthropic or humanitarian good works, conquest of markets,

military expeditions, or genocides" (40). Once again, colonial schooling had done the necessary work of censorship and self-censorship. As
soon as it was a question of *teaching* a literature—or Francophone *literatures in the plural*, as Khatibi said—that contravened the Law (of
the One), it was the *institution of the university itself*, and through it
the literary canon, the courses for the degree, and the programs that
were imposed, that would take over and make it so that there could be
no question of Francophone literature. That is, the *inter-dict* of Francophone literature, and soon its de facto inexistence, were in some way
built in, or, if one prefers, pre-programmed.

It is to this "crossing-out" of the very being of Francophone literature that I alluded when I spoke of a "scotoma" above. And to mark
with the most "visible" mark possible the blinding act of de-negation
that was, as I saw it, at work in the in-existence of this literature, I was
led to propose "crossing out" the very term "Francophonie" and to
write: ~~Francophonie~~. The "crossing-out of this word," as Heidegger said
about "being," "has only a preventive role, namely, that of preventing
the almost ineradicable habit of representing 'being' [or, in my case,
"Francophonie"] as something standing on its own."[4] One had to get
beyond this "something standing on its own" in order to begin to understand French-language literature as a concept that could not be reduced simply to meaning "literature from the Hexagon"; and at the
same time, to understand "Francophone literatures" as a concept that
could not be reduced to a "small literature," that is, a literature or literatures that "vacillate . . . between a slightly overrated glory and the
despair of only managing to create indifference."[5]

By putting an X through the lexeme "Francophonie," I also wanted
to indicate that Francophonie is not only limited to the "critical zone"
of French literature, but that it belongs to a broader *topography* that encompasses it without exhausting its potentialities. *After the fact*, I realize that it is the lack of knowledge and understanding of this *Topography of* ~~Francophonie~~ *as a concept* that "complicates" *both* French
literature *and* the so-called "Francophone" literatures, which were defined by a relation to the "center"—French literature—and that these
literatures were *in the margins*, not to say entirely marginal.[6]

---

4. I am pastiching Heidegger. See Martin Heidegger, "On the Question of Being," in
Pathmarks, trans. and ed. William McNeill (Cambridge: Cambridge University Press,
1998).
  5. Francois Pare, *Les littératures de l'exiguité* (Ottawa: Les Éditions du Nordir, 1994).
  6. Pare saw this clearly when he wrote "Until this point I have emphasized the word

What was needed was a "Topography of nihilism, of its progress, of its going beyond," in order to reach a veritable "thought of being" (Heidigger, ibid.); and it was necessary to attempt to elaborate a Topography of the "de-negation" at work in French literature, or *French-language literature,* as it used to be known, in order to begin to think the "site" of Francophone literature. The geographical, rhetorical, political, ideological, and, eventually, "memorial" sites in which this topography was inscribed had to be preceded by a *sui generis topology,* that is, by an attempt here as well to "situate this site, or place" (Heidegger, ibid.) where both purely French literature and Francophone literatures were brought together in their essence; a topology that would allow the nature of their "link" and the "site" where they were inscribed to be determined, in order to *go beyond them.*[7] This is a historical and cultural phenomenon that can only truly be "thought" by once again cutting through the false transparency of the unity of French literature "itself," and radically challenging this idea of an "itself" in the first place. Khatibi saw all of this very clearly when he linked the question of the identity of Francophone literature to a challenging of the deceptive unity of French literature. By realizing that French literature was itself shot through with multiple idioms and belongings [*appartenances*], he was already pointing to the establishment of a new topography and topology of ~~Francophonie~~.

Thus, the emergence of what has been called, somewhat vaguely

---

'small' by using a special typography, precisely in order to prevent its *fall* into a qualifier, for it seems always, whatever I do, *to lapse into a value judgment.* The same can be said of the word 'minority,' which suggests a numeric relation, but also inextricably a compatibility of values in history. *'Minority' is obviously opposed to 'majority,' but also and especially to 'priority'* (Pare, 10; except for "small," my emphasis). The same "syndrome" is at work in Jean Bernabé's, Raphaël Confiant's, and Patrick Chamoiseau's analysis of the "state of Creoleness": "The world is evolving into a state of Creoleness. The old national immovable organizations are being replaced by federations which in turn might not survive for long. Under the totalitarian universal crust, *Diversity maintained itself in small peoples, small languages, small cultures. The world standardized bristles, paradoxically, with Diversity"* (*In Praise of Creoleness,* trans. M. B. Taleb-Khyar [Baltimore: The Johns Hopkins University Press, 1990], 112).

7. One of the best descriptions of this "site" and/or "place" of theoretical inscription can be found in *In Praise of Creoleness* and in Édouard Glissant's *Caribbean Discourse, The Poetics of Relation,* and *Introduction à une poétique du divers* (Paris: Gallimard, 1996). The formulation of notions such as "creoleness" and "creolization" in their work is part of a growing awareness of the need to reconsider the very "site" of Francophonie. Glissant even goes as far as to speak of a veritable "conversion of the being" of literature in *Introduction à une poétique du divers* (15). The four lectures that make up this book are in fact devoted to this "conversion."

and off-handedly, Francophone literature (in the singular) is not, I believe, *solely* or *essentially* due to any one specific circumstance, such
as the transformation of universities, the emergence of a new audience,
a new editorial policy, a new fashion, exoticism, a desire to renew curricula, and so on. Rather, it is due to a radical disruption [*bouleverse-
ment*] of the topography of the sites of thinking and conceiving this literature as F̶r̶a̶n̶c̶o̶p̶h̶o̶n̶i̶e̶. This is the sole condition under which one
can teach French-language literature today without falling into the trap
of exoticism, folklore, or what Gayatri Spivak so aptly called "tok-
enization" and politically-correct padding! Once the dualist conception of the relation of exclusion that links French literature and Francophone literatures was eliminated, once the "veil" that made the *One*
a paragon of the Universal, and turned the *others* into substitutes for or
avatars of *"en-face"* literature—once this veil was raised, then one
could begin to read, study, and teach literatures *written in French* using a framework that no longer confined them to the catch-all category
known as "Francophonie."

This is, in any event, how I explain why it was only as of the late 1980s
that I could begin to count my work on Francophone writers as being an
integral part of my scholarship. During these years, deconstruction had
made its way in France accompanied and, in some instances, preceded
by theoretical and critical work that would greatly contribute to a better understanding of the at times hybrid, at times multiple or diverse
character of this new "site" or "place" that F̶r̶a̶n̶c̶o̶p̶h̶o̶n̶i̶e̶ was to become—a "site," a "place" that would finally allow the sketching out of
possible ways to go beyond the nihilism at work in the *dogmatic,* not to
say frankly "metaphysical," concept of Francophonie. I am thinking of
course of the emergence and consolidation of feminist studies, and the
subsequent rise of cultural and postcolonial studies. Each of these
movements of critical thought, because it had allowed a profound rethinking of the relations of inequality, hierarchy, subjection, and domination, contributed directly or indirectly to an awareness of the importance of Francophone literature within the broader framework of
literary studies and, more specifically, within the framework of so-
called "subaltern" studies. It was this work that allowed the Topography in question to be "drawn" and the main parameters of the new
Topology "F̶r̶a̶n̶c̶o̶p̶h̶o̶n̶i̶e̶" to be marked out.

When I moved from UVA to Brown in 1992, the entire intellectual
landscape of academia had changed, and it was obvious that the literature with which I had been involved almost clandestinely for years

could find its place in the curriculum. As I have tried to show—even if I have had to go against certain norms of theoretical *exposure* and in so doing "expose" myself—the essential condition of possibility for the inclusion of this literature in the curriculum is not *only* of a factual order. But it is only with full knowledge of the facts underlying the *problematic* nature of the "site" where it had been in a sense "lodged" that ~~Francophonie~~ could at last emerge as a literature that had to be taken into account if one wanted to understand the nature of the contradictions, confrontations, misunderstandings, and other "identity crises" that have put their mark on French literature and Francophone literatures. And, in this sense, Khatibi was right when he stated that "it is an entirely new and essential situation" with which one is faced when dealing with texts belonging to the category that had been called "small literatures." This "situation"—or, if one prefers, this "site"—has revealed to us that to practice ~~Francophonie~~ today is, in effect, to bring "into play not only French literature, but in a radical way, the French language as a principle of identity." But this is also to challenge, in an equally radical way, the "general economy"—hierarchies, identities, transfers, and cultural, historical, political, and ideological intertexts, as well as the *languages* [*idiomes*]—that governed the ~~inscription~~ of so-called Francophone literatures in our curriculum.

Today, Francophone (without the X this time!) literature seems to have adapted, become accepted. Some tell us that it has been "integrated" and that it is now a part of world literatures, or that it is a literature "in its own right." We know, however, that as long as it is judged in comparison to the literature of *"en face,"* it has very little hope of truly existing and this, no matter what share it is given. Still, I can say that for many of our colleagues it remains a marginal literature that they continue to view as the *shadow* of French literature; they speak of a passing fad and are waiting, more or less patiently, for it to "pass" as other fads have. To do so, however, is not to fully appreciate the "transition," to have no idea of the nature of the "site" that this literature occupies with increasing confidence. To do so is to admit that one has not yet become aware of the "site" from where, *from all times*, it had silently begun to cut into the self-transparency of the literature from which it was said to stem. To do so is to say that the fortress is still holding up. We know, however, that the small breach that has been opened is not about to close again.

—Translated by Alyson Waters

KAREN L. GOULD

Nationalism, Feminism, Cultural Pluralism: American Interest in Quebec Literature and Culture

THE RISE OF INTEREST IN FRENCH-SPEAKING CANADA

Over the past three decades American academic interest in the Francophone culture of Quebec has continued to grow, despite the relatively small population (7 million) of the predominantly French-speaking province and despite general American disinterest in our Canadian neighbors to the North. Courses that explore Quebec literature and culture have been taught successfully for nearly thirty years at northeastern institutions such as Colby College, Dartmouth College, SUNY-Plattsburgh, University of Connecticut, University of Maine, and the University of Vermont. When the Northeast Council for Quebec Studies was formed in 1981, its very name underscored the organization's primarily regional character, reflecting the historical cross-border ties between New England and Quebec. A decade later, data published by the Association for Canadian Studies in the United States indicated that 35 four-year colleges and 48 public and private universities in states as far away as Florida, Virginia, Ohio, Illinois, Colorado, California, and Washington, offer courses on French-Canadian literature and culture.[1]

Anticipating a broadening interest in French Canada and Quebec in particular, the Northeast Council for Quebec Studies changed its name in 1984 to the American Council for Quebec Studies, and its biannual publication, *Quebec Studies,* has become the leading American journal devoted to French-Canadian culture and Quebec letters. Interest in Quebec literature has also been spurred by the geographical proximity of French-speaking Canada, political independence issues in

1. *A Profile of Canadian Studies* (Washington, D.C.: ACSUS, 1991).

YFS 103, *French and Francophone,* ed. Farid Laroussi and Christopher L. Miller, © 2003 by Yale University.

Quebec, and the many Francophone cultural opportunities available for American faculty and students who choose to study in Quebec or in other parts of French-speaking Canada.

In the United States, scholarship on French-Canadian literature and culture has grown, appearing in a variety of journals and American academic presses as well. At the same time, American scholarship on French-Canadian literature now appears regularly in prominent Canadian journals such as *Canadian Literature, Canadian Theatre Review, Essays on Canadian Writing, Études littéraires, Jeu, Journal of Canadian Studies, Studies in Canadian Literature,* and *Voix et images.* This cross-border dialogue among Canadian and American scholars has become increasingly rich.

CHALLENGING THE FRENCH CANON

The insertion of French-Canadian literature and culture into the curriculum of traditional French programs has been met with a range of positive and less positive responses. As with the new curriculum on African and Caribbean Francophone studies, the primary challenge has been the encounter with French canonical thinking. Some colleagues have been unable to conceive of French-Canadian letters and culture as anything other than the folkloric "deformation" of the mother culture. This point of view invariably positions Francophone cultural production in Quebec on the periphery of French studies; it presumes, moreover, that the Francophone world is inherently provincial, situated outside the real center of cultural and economic power (France), and therefore academically suspect. As such, both the Francophone object of study and the sociocultural space to which this "other" object of study relates remain marginalized and colonized.

As with other Francophone literatures, the issue of what to do with French-Canadian literature has been part of a recent, much broader ideological debate about the institutional and cultural power of literary canons in general. In the case of French programs in the United States, this debate has inevitably raised questions about the authority of the French literary canon over program curricula, much the way the expansion of American literature curricula would challenge the dominance of British letters in English departments of the 1960s. For colleagues whose careers have focused exclusively on French literature and culture, the arrival of Francophone studies has often been viewed as the inevitable introduction of the "minority" voice, which can be welcomed as long as dominant assumptions are not challenged. One or two additional courses on Francophone topics are now more easily accepted than in the past and comprehensive exam lists may include Francophone authors. However, Francophone studies in the plural are still commonly viewed as ancillary to the "core" mission of the traditional French program.

Once a "Francophone hire" has been made, the new faculty member is often expected to "cover" the entire French-speaking world outside France—this was my experience when I was hired at Virginia Polytechnic Institute and State University in 1980 and again at Bowling Green State University in 1985. Yet as Christiane Makward pointed out over a decade ago, "the term 'Francophone' is to be decoded skeptically"[2] in the Academy, especially since the term "Francophone" is a homogenizing designation that necessarily flattens out historical and cultural differences across diverse national and ethnic groups. In addition, the term "Francophone" may perpetuate the legacy of colonialism that has over-emphasized the French language as *the* umbilical cord to the mother culture, resulting in misconceptions about the indigenous culture and its complex relations with European cultural traditions. Indeed, debates over issues of French language usage in Quebec, the Caribbean, and in African countries where French is spoken have raised important theoretical and political questions about the very term "Francophone."

The administrative challenge of determining how to expand the curricular focus of French programs with new Francophone positions has been complicated by the very real problem of declining or, at best, flat French enrollments at many U.S. institutions. As tenure-track positions in French dwindle, department heads have fewer opportunities to make significant curricular transformations. Recognizing at the same time that Francophone studies is a complex field, an increasing number of institutions have acknowledged that one Francophone position is not sufficient.

POLITICAL APPEAL OF "QUÉBÉCOIS" WRITING

Like a number of American critics of my generation who were drawn to the study of Quebec letters due to the intriguing political and cultural debates emerging in Quebec during the 1960s, my own interest in

2. Christiane Makward, "The Others' Others: 'Francophone' Women and Writing" *Yale French Studies* 75 (1988): 191.

Quebec writing and culture was initially spurred by the significant role minority politics and political discourse have played in the literature and culture of Quebec. Since the Quiet Revolution of the early 1960s, critical discussions of Quebec literature and culture have often been articulated against the backdrop of Quebec nationalism (*"la question nationale"*) and Francophone identity politics. Connections between Quebec nationalist ideology and cultural production have become transparent in much of the social theory and literary criticism produced in Quebec since the 1970s. A number of Canadian and American critics have in fact argued that the overarching themes of Quebec writing are invariably linked to the aspirations of Quebec nationalism and the desire for political independence.[3] As one of the primary markers of Quebec's historical difference in North America, the survival of the French language—and along with it the politics of linguistic identity—has indeed been a crucial theme around which collective identity politics have been forged in French Canada since the British Conquest in 1759. The strong French language legislation in effect in Quebec today, which promotes *francisation* in the workplace and the public schools, has its roots in the burning political debates of the 1960s and 1970s over the use of French in Quebec,[4] debates that I encountered during my first visit to Montreal in 1976 in the department stores, on city streets, and in the media and literature of the time.

The decade of the 1970s was an era of strong nationalist activity in Quebec, accompanied by a vigorous cultural affirmation of Francophone identity. The magnetism of Quebec's Francophone nationalist landscape would attract a number of American scholars of my generation to Quebec letters and to the works of a group of writers such as Hubert Aquin, Jacques Godbout, Jacques Ferron, Gaston Miron, Michèle Lalonde, Gérard Godin, and others, who consciously sought to politicize the literary construction of a national "Québécois" identity. Quebec nationalists began using the term "Québécois" instead of "French Canadian" to focus public attention on the distinctiveness of the Francophone experience in Quebec. This decision understandably angered minority populations of Francophone Canadians outside Quebec (especially in Ontario, Nova Scotia, and New Brunswick) who felt abandoned by the political agenda of Québécois nationalism and, more

3. Jacques Pelletier, *Lecture politique du roman québécois contemporain* (Montreal: Université du Québec à Montréal, 1984).
4. See Mark Levine, *The Reconquest of Montreal: Language Policy and Social Change in a Bilingual City* (Philadelphia: Temple University Press, 1990).

28   *Yale French Studies*

specifically, the aspiration of the Parti Québécois to separate from the "rest of Canada."

When examining modern Quebec literature and culture, the discourses of decolonization and postcolonialism have been especially useful. In this regard, the discourse of decolonization articulated in the works of Franz Fanon, Albert Memmi, and Aimé Césaire, for example, has proved particularly valuable for understanding important theoretical underpinnings in Quebec writing. For many American scholars of Quebec literature, the lure of Quebec letters is to some degree linked to a fascination with the minority political aspirations of a French-speaking population on a continent dominated by English-speaking political, economic, and cultural power.

QUEBEC WOMEN WRITERS AND
NORTH AMERICAN FEMINISM

In a 1993 assessment of trends in American scholarship on Quebec literature since 1970, Jane Moss remarks that

> the most striking aspect of the growth of Quebec literary criticism in the United States during the 1980s was the explosion of feminist scholarship. Well versed in the semiotic, linguistic, and psychoanalytic theories of French feminists (Kristeva, Cixous, Irigaray, Hermann, Yaguello), and the sociological, philosophical, and poetic theories of American feminists (Chodorow, Dinnerstein, Daly, Rich), numerous scholars have explored contemporary women's writing and theater, and have unearthed or reinterpreted women's writing of the past.[5]

Among American scholars of Quebec literature, critical interest in Quebec's most well-known women writers (Gabrielle Roy, Marie-Claire Blais, Anne Hébert, Nicole Brossard) has been substantial. Significant critical discussion has also been given to the works of Denise Boucher, France Théoret, Louky Bersianik, Madeleine Gagnon, Jovette Marchessault, Francine Noël, Monique LaRue, Madeleine Monette, Marie Laberge, Louise Dupré, and others.

The plethora of publications by U.S.-based scholars on Quebec women writers has been noteworthy and indicative of keen scholarly interest in both Francophone women's writing and feminist issues in

5. Jane Moss, "Studies on Literature in French: From 'Meagerness' to 'Modified Rapture,'" *Northern Exposures: Scholarship on Canada in the United States*, ed. Karen Gould, Joseph T. Jockel, and William Metcalfe (Washington, D.C.: Association for Canadian Studies in the United States, 1993), 241–69.

Quebec. Over the past two decades, numerous books, edited collections, journal articles, and essays have appeared, confirming Jane Moss's observation that women writing in Quebec have attracted serious scholarly interest and discussion among feminist critics in the U.S. On the other side of the border, Anglophone and Francophone critics in Canada have also been critically engaged in the assessment of women's writings in Quebec and in other provinces of Canada. My own research on Quebec women writers has been influenced by scholarship on both sides of the border, including Paula Gilbert Lewis's path-breaking collection, *Traditionalism, Nationalism, and Feminism: Women Writers of Quebec,* Mary Jean Green's study of Marie-Claire Blais, Patricia Smart's *Écrire dans la maison du père,* Gilbert and Dufault's *Doing Gender: Franco-Canadian Women Writers of the 1990s,* and Mary Jean Green's recent examination of *Women and Narrative Identity: Rewriting the Quebec National Text.*[6]

For American critics with a background in French and North American feminisms, the attraction of Quebec women's writings since the mid-1970s is easy to understand. Inspired by and participating in an increasingly influential women's movement in Quebec, a number of women writers have challenged conventional literary structures and developed themes and poetic lexicons designed to affirm women's experience and independence beyond the domestic sphere. Experimental writers such as Nicole Brossard, Louky Bersianik, Madeleine Gagnon, France Théoret, Jovette Marchessault, and Louise Dupré have endeavored to construct a female subject no longer dependent on male-oriented norms for legitimacy or agency. For Brossard, Bersianik, Gagnon, Théoret, Marchessault, and Dupré, *"écriture au féminin"* has been "their response to a historic moment of radical cultural re-assessment, signaling the first steps in a period of transition from a patriarchal to a more egalitarian society, from a notion of sexuality based on reproduction and commodification to an understanding of sexuality that incorporates the polyvalent, fluctuating, and regenerative aspects of the fe-

6. *Traditionalism, Nationalism, and Feminism: Women Writers of Quebec,* ed. Paula Gilbert Lewis (Westport, Conn: Greenwood, 1985); Mary Jean Green, *Marie-Claire Blais* (New York: Twayne Publications, 1995); Patricia Smart, *Écrire dans la maison du père* (Montreal: Québec/Amérique, 1988); *Doing Gender: Franco-Canadian Women Writers of the 1990s,* ed. Paula Ruth Gilbert and Roseanna L. Dufault (Cranbury, New Jersey: Farleigh Dickinson University Press, 2001); and Mary Jean Green, *Women and Narrative Identity: Rewriting the Quebec National Text* (Montreal: McGill-Queen's University Press, 2001).

male body, its passion and its knowledge."[7] Often, these writers have turned away from the traditional patriarchal family, which has exerted historic control in rural, Catholic Quebec, toward the modern urban sphere in their efforts to imagine a more creative, more liberatory space for women.

American scholarship on Quebec women's writings has emphasized the contributions of contemporary Quebec women writers to the changing social and literary discourse on female subjecthood in North America. It has also reviewed the project of Quebec nationalism and collective identity construction with fresh perspectives, aligning issues of cultural marginality, economic exploitation, and ethnic difference with gender politics, subordination in domestic life, and women's need for self-determination. As Mary Jean Green notes, a number of Quebec women authors have written against the nostalgia and virilization of nationalist discourse in the novels of male writers in the 1960s and 70s, and have proposed instead "their own rewritings of Quebec identity, interrogating older constructions of narrative, of history, of nationalism, and of identity itself, and extending the definition of Quebec identity beyond the monolithic *pure laine* masculine subject to encompass the plural, even pluricultural identities that have come to constitute postreferendum, postmodern Quebec."[8] American scholarship has also examined geographical and cultural displacements throughout North America in the works of contemporary Quebec women writers and has thus broadened the impact of Quebec women's writings on the status of women and men in contemporary culture.[9]

CULTURAL PLURALISM AND QUEBEC LETTERS

In the 1980s and '90s, debates within Quebec society over inclusive versus exclusive approaches to collective identity construction, and over the politics of cultural sovereignty versus cultural assimilation, have generated further interest in the forms of nationalist discourse circu-

7. Karen Gould, *Writing in the Feminine* (Carbondale: Southern Illinois University Press, 1990), 49.

8. Green, *Women and Narrative Identity*, 20.

9. Gould, "Rewriting 'America': Violence, Postmodernity, and Parody in the Fiction of Madeleine Monette, Nicole Brossard, and Monique LaRue," in *Postcolonial Subjects: Francophone Women Writers*, ed. Mary Jean Green, Karen Gould, Micheline Rice-Maximin, Keith L. Walker, and Jack A. Yeager, (Minneapolis: University of Minnesota Press, 1996), 189.

lating in Quebec since the 1960s. These debates have become central in the works of a number of contemporary Quebec writers, including immigrant writers such as Régine Robin, Flora Balzano, Dany Laferrière, Marco Micone, and Ying Chen, and central as well to scholarly discussions on contemporary Francophone writing and culture in Quebec. Over the last decade, American scholarship has to some degree moved beyond Quebec nationalism and beyond the cultural borders of Quebec as well to explore Franco-Ontarion letters and drama, Acadian writers, affiliations with Louisiana history and culture, cross-cultural comparisons with Francophone writers from other countries, and connections with the birth cultures of Quebec's recent immigrants from Central Europe, Latin America and the Caribbean, and Asia. As a result, issues of immigrant urban culture, plurilingualism, ethnic diversity, cultural *métissage,* transculturalism, and *américanité* ("North American-ness") have been identified as powerful themes in recent Quebec writing. In the context of a post-referendum Quebec and an increasingly diverse Montreal, reflecting on the distinctiveness of Francophone literature in Quebec raises new questions about writing and collective identity in North America.[10]

Addressing issues of cultural *métissage* and the blending of ethnic differences, recent texts by Quebec immigrant writers have prompted considerable critical attention both in Canada and the U.S. For instance, Régine Robin's *La Québécoite* has been the subject of a number of critical studies that explore the shifting terrain of ethnic identity politics in contemporary Montreal, against the historical backdrop of European Jewish persecution. Robin's dialectical stance in *La Québécoite* insists on a plurality of voices and an explosion of social codes and national identities in an intercultural narrative that bridges the political and social histories of two continents. In the works of Régine Robin, Flora Balzano, Mona Latif Ghatttas, Nadine Ltaif, Dany Laferrière, Marco Micone, and Ying Chen, writing is no longer defined in terms of a "unified" Francophone culture, no longer characterized by a national discourse that seeks to erase or polarize intracultural difference. As Robert Schwartzwald notes,

> Quebec writing has come to increasingly situate itself such that the dichotomy it addresses is no longer between English and French, whether understood as languages or as cultures in a majority/minority Canadian

---

10. See Pierre Nepveu, *L'Écologie du réel. Mort et naissance de la littérature québécoise contemporaine* (Montreal: Boréal, 1988).

context. Instead, it explores the heterogeneity of language in Québec itself, including interactions among world languages and confrontations
between different registers of French.[11]

American scholarship on Quebec literarture and culture has continued
to grow, due in large measure to critical interest in the discourses of nationalism, feminism, postcolonialism, minority identity construction,
and global Francophone studies. With respect to feminist theory and
international women's writings, Quebec literature has proven to be an
especially rich field of inquiry. By the same token, the study of Quebec
literature and culture, like Francophone studies more broadly speaking, offers American students the opportunity to reflect on the cultural
differences and collective identity politics that circulate in the texts of
North American authors for whom living and writing in French continue to matter.

11. Robert Schwartzwald, "An/other Canada. Another Canada? Other Canadas,"
The Massachusetts Review (Spring/Summer 1990): 16.

SAMBA GADJIGO

Teaching Francophone African
Literature in the American Academy

Concluding the introduction to his book *Literary Theory: An Introduction*, a work that has become indispensable for teachers and students of literature, Terry Eagleton wrote:

> What we have uncovered so far, then, . . . is that the value-judgments
> by which [literature] is constituted are themselves historically variable,
> but that these value-judgments themselves have a close relation to so-
> cial ideologies. They refer in the end not simply to private taste, but to
> the assumptions by which certain social groups exercise and maintain
> power over others.[1]

The genesis of the American university system and the important
transformations that it has experienced during its history confirm
what may be obvious: that there have always been close links between
universities and the larger forces that control American society as a
whole. Looking more broadly still, numerous examples would support
the idea that everywhere in the world, the university has been con-
trolled by those who hold power within society. That is perhaps the
only thing that is "universal" about a university.

Starting from that premise, this essay will seek to contribute to the
debate on the place given to the teaching of Francophone African literature (or literatures) in American academies. This will be less a scientific survey of the question than a sketch of the present state of things.
A decade has elapsed since the publication of Adrien Huannou's book
*La critique et l'enseignement de la littérature africaine aux États-
Unis*,[2] and it has been forty years since the first entrance of Franco-

1. Terry Eagleton, *Literary Theory: An Introduction* (Minneapolis: University of
Minnesota Press, 1983), 16.
2. Adrien Huannou, *La critique et l'enseignement de la littérature africaine aux
États-Unis* (Paris: L'Harmattan, 1993).

YFS 103, *French and Francophone*, ed. Farid Laroussi and Christopher L. Miller,
© 2003 by Yale University.

phone African literature into the American academy. The catalogues and programs of numerous American colleges and universities, the growing number of experts, teachers, and professional associations, the increase in publications and in study abroad programs all show that great progress has been made in the teaching of Africa. However, a closer look at the status of Africa within American academic culture reveals that, in spite of the presence of experts and eager students, Francophone African literature is far from having the status of a discipline; it remains instead a marginal specialization.

In this essay I discuss when, how, and why the Francophone literature of Africa appeared within the American university system. What was at stake? Who made this happen, and within what context?

What we call Francophone African literature dates only from the years following World War I, the first text being *Les trois volontés de Malic,* a novella published in 1920 by the Senegalese teacher Ahmadou Mapaté Diagne.[3] And it was only from the 1960s through the 1980s that this literature made its first timid advances as a specialty in the programs of American universities, under the aegis of departments of French. It is to be noted that, in the same period, this literature was marginalized in the new universities of Francophone Africa itself, where it was also set up under the tutelage of departments of French or modern literature.

As Adrien Huannou has pointed out, it was in 1966, with the advent of the Black Power movement led by Stokely Carmichael and the awakening of historical and cultural awareness among African Americans, that black America turned toward African Studies. The desegregation of many American universities between 1970 and 1973 increased access to higher education for black students, and interest in African literature rose. Departments and programs of Black Studies increased from 350 to 600 in less than three years. Before examining the reception and evolution of Francophone African literature within these movements of the 1970s and 1980s, I would like to bring in the contrasting example of the social sciences and their role in African Studies in the United States.

In the decade following World War II, some measure of interest in Africa and African Studies already existed in a small number of insti-

---

3. Ahmadou Mapaté Diagne, *Les trois volontés de Malic* (Nendeln: Kraus Reprints, 1973).

tutions. Thus, for example, well before the burgeoning of Black Studies, a few institutions, including the Hartford Theological Seminary, offered courses in African languages. In 1951 at Northwestern University, the cultural anthropologist Melville J. Herskovits founded the first program of African Studies at an American university. At Indiana University, theses were being written on Africanist subjects, and starting in 1965 African languages including Fula, Wolof, Kiswahili, and Bamanankan were offered, as were other courses in the African social sciences. In 1953 the Ford Foundation financed at Boston University a Foreign Area Program that included African Studies; the African Studies Center at the University of California at Los Angeles was founded by James S. Coleman in 1959 and is today one of the most important in the world. Before 1960 most courses on Africa originated in departments of anthropology or programs in geography. It should be noted also that, along with the initiatives of the Ford Foundation and the Mellon Foundation, the United States government itself has supported the study of Africa through the Title VI program, under the rubric of "uncommon languages and cultures."[4]

In 1957, the founding of the African Studies Association brought together Africanist scholars and teachers, most of whom were in the social sciences; this event marked the "official" birth of African Studies in the United States. If space permitted it would be interesting to explore the reasons for the lag between the social sciences and the humanities: why did departments of language and literature wait until the end of the 1960s—or even much later—before they finally took an interest in European-language African literatures? Why was Africa somehow more important to the social sciences than to the humanities?

It was in fact near the end of the 1960s that African literature written in French first entered the American academy, under the wing of departments of French. This happened as the result of the initiatives of a number of isolated individuals. According to Thomas Cassirer, a retired professor of African literature at the University of Massachusetts at Amherst, one of the earliest pioneers was Mercer Cook, an African-American professor of French at Howard University. After meeting Léopold S. Senghor at the first Congress of Black Writers and Artists in Paris in 1956, Cook began teaching Senghor's poetry at Howard.[5] From

4. For more information about the study of Africa in the United States before the rise of African Studies programs per se, see Peter Duignan and L. H. Gann, *The United States and Africa: A History* (Cambridge: Cambridge University Press, 1984).
5. Interview with Thomas Cassirer, Amherst, October 2001.

that point forward, the teaching of Francophone African literature advanced by tiny steps, in rare French departments where the general condescension toward the former colonies could be partially overcome. Thus Emile Snyder arrived at the University of Wisconsin at Madison in 1963 and launched the first initiative in Francophone African literature there; thus Thomas Cassirer taught the first course on this literature at "UMass" in 1966.

The case of this particular pioneer demonstrates how African literature was obliged to "infiltrate" French departments in American universities. Cassirer earned his Ph.D. in nineteenth- and twentieth-century French literature from Yale in 1960 and began his career at Smith College. The pathbreaking role of Smith within French studies is confirmed by the fact that it founded one of the very first study abroad programs in France in 1924. Even more remarkable is the fact that before 1960, Smith offered fellowships to faculty members for the study and teaching of African literature; however, there were no takers. Professor Cassirer admits that it was only under the influence of a colleague in anthropology at Smith that he discovered African literature, in 1964. That same year, the Ford Foundation offered fellowships to professors of French interested in acquainting themselves with African texts and introducing them into their courses. The rising demands of black students for a curriculum that would reflect their roots and their identity—within universities that remained focused on the classics—undoubtedly contributed to the sudden "opening" onto Francophone Africa. Hoping to pursue his interest in African literature and share it with students, Cassirer left Smith in 1965 for the University of Massachusetts. As a state university, "UMass" was sensitive to political pressures; Cassirer offered the first course on Francophone African literature on the Amherst campus in 1966, the same year in which the first Festival of Black Arts took place in Dakar, Senegal.

The arrival of African literature in my department of French at Mount Holyoke College in 1970 was the work of Émile Langlois, a professor from France and a specialist of French literature; his was the only course offered until 1984, when the department decided to hire an Africanist.

Another case worthy of attention is that of the department of French at the University of Illinois at Champaign-Urbana. Until 1982, only one professor out of the dozen in the department offered a course on North Africa; another taught courses on Quebec literature. For students who were interested in majoring in Francophone literature of

North Africa and Sub-Saharan Africa, the department offered the possibility of an "Expanded French Studies"—without real supervision. This meant that the very few students who devoted themselves to African literature were largely left to themselves; this situation lasted well into the 1980s.

It is easy to imagine the handicap faced by the few graduate students who came to these institutions from Francophone Africa, faced with this lack of structure. But the situation they left behind in Africa was not terribly different. Indeed, we should take the case of what is now called the Université Cheikh Anta Diop de Dakar, the national university of Senegal. Opened in 1959, this university had a School of Letters and Social Sciences that contained a department of modern literature (*lettres modernes*). Until 1982, the backbone of that department was the study of French language and literature, taking the lion's share of courses, staff, and resources. Lilyan Kesteloot of the Institut Fondamental d'Afrique Noire was the sole specialist of African oral literature; Francophone poetry was taught by Sylvia Washington Ba alone. In the whole department, Francophone African fiction was taught by only one assistant professor. Aside from this dearth of specialists, the near-total absence of bibliographical resources made real research practically impossible; the field further suffered from a lack of theoretical and methodological courses. These problems were compounded by the population explosion among students in the 1970s and 1980s: the demands of teaching so many students left the professors no time to advance the research that would help to ground the field. This ironic situation in an African university was further exacerbated by the fact that the only centers for research in African literature were located in France; the absence of subsidies made access to these resources inaccessible to all but a few Senegalese scholars. In the light of this situation at the University of Dakar, the least one can say is that its students were poorly prepared to enter Ph.D. programs at research universities.

It should be mentioned also, as the case of Thomas Cassirer illustrates, that until the 1970s or even later, all those who initiated courses on Francophone literature were, so to speak, self-taught. The training of the first generation of specialists who took the lead in the 1980s was thus the work of these exceptional "volunteers."

Where do we stand now? What status does "Francophone" Africa have in the American academy? Certainly many departments of French can fairly claim to have (finally) opened their doors to teaching and research on French-language literatures outside France. Many have renamed themselves departments of French "and Francophone" studies. Beside the growth in the number of departments that have been liberal enough to grant a place to this literature in their curriculum, the field has benefited from the emergence of two institutions: a journal and an association. The journal *Research in African Literatures* was founded in 1970 and has provided an important channel for debates about African literatures in many languages. But a rapid review of the essays published in its first issue shows that interest in Anglophone countries dominated; this slant is still visible in volume 31, number 3 (fall 2000), despite the two special sections on Ahmadou Hampaté Ba and Sony Labou Tansi. The creation of the African Literature Association in 1974 provided another important forum for thought. The progress that has been made and the growth of the field can be measured in the membership rolls of the African Literature Association, which grew from 17 founding members to 500 in 1985.[6]

As I suggested earlier, greater numbers of departments of French have begun to teach African texts in the last ten years. A surge of interest in Francophone literatures was reflected in the Modern Language Association's *Joblist* in the 1990s; for several years, as departments sought to diversify their offerings, Francophone positions seemed to dominate the listings. The rich bibliography, including more than 400 titles, compiled by Adrien Huannou in 1993, showed the extensive progress that had already been made by that date.[7] It is also noteworthy that a section on African literature has been included in the MLA *Bibliography* since 1968. And without doubt, since the publication in 1986 of the groundbreaking critical volume *Ngambika: Studies of Women in African Literature*, there has been a growing interest in the writings of African women, even if one must regret that Mariama Bâ was the only Francophone author in that collection.[8]

Still, in spite of these undeniable signs of progress, it must be rec-

6. For more details on the evolution of the reception and teaching of African literatures in American universities up to 1985, see Stephen Arnold, ed., *African Literature Studies: The Present State/L'État présent* (Washington, D.C.: Three Continents Press, 1985). In his essay in that volume, "African Literary Studies: The Emergence of a New Discipline," Arnold analyzes the entire infrastructure (anthologies, guides, other publications and organizations) that supported the emergence of African literature.

7. Huannou, *La critique et l'enseignement*, 171–222. It should be noted that this bibliography includes works on Francophone, Anglophone, and Lusophone literatures.

8. Carole Boyce Davies and Anne Adams Graves, *Ngambika: Studies of Women in African Literature* (Trenton: African World Press, 1986).

ognized that within most French departments, the study and teaching of African literature remains quite marginal, in terms of both the resources that are allotted to it and the role to which it is assigned in the curriculum. How much has really changed? In 1976, Bernth Lindfors wrote: "African literature is a specialty rather than a discipline in American universities, and it appears destined to remain so for the foreseeable future. . . . Until these deficiencies are remedied, African literature is not likely to gain recognition as a separate but equal humanistic discipline in American academia."[9] Thomas Hale and Richard Priebe reinforced this idea, writing: "The teacher of African literature is too often an isolated individual, one who must single-handedly convey an appreciation of the verbal art of an entire continent to both students and colleagues."[10]

As for the present, a glance at the catalogues and faculty rosters of almost any French department now confirms that little has changed. A couple of examples will suffice. At the University of Massachusetts at Amherst, the position in Francophone literature disappeared ten years ago, the victim of budget cuts. In an institution as well off as Harvard, the department of Romance Languages and Literatures has nearly 30 teachers, with 12 in the French section; one person alone covers all of the literature (not to mention cinema) of Francophone Africa. In Brown University's Department of French Studies, which includes 13 members, there is only one specialist of the Maghreb, and that specialization is combined with the literature and theory of the twentieth century. The burden that is placed on the specialist of Francophone African literature is compounded by the frequent practice, for budgetary reasons, of demanding that the literature of the Caribbean be taught by the same person as well.

Often isolated within a French department, the Africanist is rarely a professor of literature itself; he cannot teach his texts as his colleagues do, emphasizing their artistic value. Most often, in a context where Africa remains *terra incognita*, he must provide a background in geography, history, anthropology, and political science—all of which is necessary as a basis for understanding the creation of a work of art. Whatever his or her nationality might be, the specialist of African literature is often expected to represent all of Africa.

9. Berth Lindfors, "On Disciplining Students in a Nondiscipline," in Thomas Hale and Richard Priebe, eds., *The Teaching of African Literature* (Washington, D.C.: Three Continents Press, 1989): 41.

10. Hale and Priebe, eds., *The Teaching of African Literature*, viii.

Thus, we can see that great progress has been made in terms of the number of positions opened and in the number of departments that have begun to include Francophone African literature. In a related phenomenon, there has been considerable growth in the ranks of specialists and in the field of publishing. Judging from the number of study abroad programs for undergraduates in, for example, Senegal and Niger, as well as from enrollments in courses in general, it is obvious that students' interest in this literature has expanded significantly. However, within departments and institutions, the role that is played by this literature and the financial and human resources that are devoted to it leave much to be desired and much still to be done. For, as Bernth Lindfors remarked: "Among the extracurricular factors inhibiting the orderly growth of African literature study in the United States are overt and covert racism, widespread ignorance of all things African, shrinking university budgets, . . . and deep institutional inertia."[11]

—Translated by Christopher L. Miller

11. Lindfors, "On Disciplining Students in a Nondiscipline," 41.

II. Configurations of French and Francophone around the World

DANIEL DELAS

Francophone Literary Studies in France: Analyses and Reflections

The distinction between "French" and "Francophone" whose existence is pointed out by the very title of this volume is the object of a
longstanding debate in France. In the 1980s, one frequently heard
African poets and novelists vehemently refusing to be categorized as
"Francophone" writers when they considered themselves to be entirely "French" writers. Similarly, many of the big bookstores refused
for a long time to create a section devoted to "Francophone" writers
who would then be subcategorized by geographical regions: Caribbean,
Africa, the Mascarene Islands. The argument most often used to justify
this practice was the danger of ghettoization, of creating a *de facto* sub-
category and thus relegating Francophone literature to the status of a
subliterature (like regional literature, popular literature, mysteries,
and so on). Was this the fear of a minority that no longer is a minority,
at least not to the same extent? The fact is, the debate does seem to have
lost some of its acuity and bitterness, and the "Francophone" category
is used today with less neurosis. This is no doubt because it has taken
on more importance, has affirmed itself, has come into its own; its
"French" legitimacy is no longer in question. In any case, the new curricula for the last two years of French high school freely use the distinction between "French" and "Francophone," which amounts to a
sort of official dubbing of the harmonious coexistence of the two terms
in official French vocabulary. And in the major bookstores, the existence of tables or sections that classify "Francophone" writers by geographical region is the rule at this point, be it at the FNAC, at Gibert,
or in the big provincial bookstores.

In the following brief presentation, I shall first attempt to describe
the status of Francophone literatures in secondary school and university curricula; I shall then put forth a few more general explanatory hy-

YFS 103, *French and Francophone,* ed. Farid Laroussi and Christopher L. Miller,
© 2003 by Yale University.

43

potheses. This piece is thus a survey of the lay of the land followed by a reflection on *why* things are as they are and not on *how* one should teach Francophone literature, an area in which there already exist serious methodological reflections that can be consulted.[1]

THE STATUS OF THE TEACHING OF FRANCOPHONE LITERATURES IN THE FRENCH EDUCATIONAL SYSTEM

The reputation of the centralization of French education is long-established: for a long time, everything was decided from on high, and the loosening of the Napoleonic stranglehold did not begin until the second half of the twentieth century, gradually allowing teachers a certain autonomy. Teachers of French[2] (language and literature) are divided into schoolteachers (elementary school), middle and high school teachers (secondary school), and university professors. Much more so than in the United States, these teachers share a common training, having attended the same educational institutions (universities and university institutes for the training of teachers) and sometimes having taken the same examinations (the *CAPES* and especially the *agrégation*). Many university professors have taught in secondary schools and many teachers who have doctorates and have not found positions at the university level teach in high schools. It is also important to remember that secondary school teaching includes the so-called "preparatory" classes, which are university level (with, in addition, a highly select group of students).[3]

1. For example, in *Perspectives actuelles de l'enseignement du français* (Ministère de l'Education Nationale, CRDP de l'Académie de Versailles, 2001), the acts of an important national seminar that took place on 23–25 October 2000, organized by Alain Boissinot, there are two good articles on the question of how to teach: Jean-Louis Joubert, "Francophonies et l'enseignement du français," and Christiane Chaulet-Achour, "Francophonies."

2. There is a very French debate concerning what to call teachers in this field. Without going as far as the totally obsolete term "professor of humanities," tradition dictated that they be called "professor of letters," as an echo of the examinations they took (the *CAPES* or the *agrégation*), exams in either "classical letters" or "modern letters." This usage has faded away and one speaks these days of a "professor of French," specifying, if need be, "language and literature" in parenthesis. The "progressive" association of teachers of French is called the AFEF (Association Française des Enseignants de Français), but its more traditional rival is called the APL (Association des Professeurs de Lettres). It's as if a battle of ideas must always start out as a battle of words!

3. This is another professional debate that is difficult for people outside the French system to understand: the opposition between the elite tracks and the ordinary tracks.

This explains why, in order to get an even vaguely accurate idea of the status of Francophone literary studies, it is appropriate to take a two-pronged approach, first looking at the secondary-school level and then at the university level.

Secondary School Teaching

The curricula of middle and high schools were updated extensively in the 1990s. As far as middle schools are concerned, the *Instructions* of 1977, followed by those of 1985, were characterized by a desire for openness that would take into account the heterogeneity of the students, an openness to communication and to a diversity of linguistic registers and, in the area that interests us here, to Francophone authors. On the list of recommended authors, one thus sees the appearance in 1985 (according to the 14 November decree) of four Francophone works: *Les contes d'Amadou Coumba* and *Les nouveaux contes* (Birago Diop); *L'enfant noir* (Camara Laye); *Les bouts de bois de Dieu* (Ousmane Sembene); and *Nedjma* (Kateb Yacine). An interesting start, even if *Nedjma* is perhaps too ambitious for middle school students. In order to encourage teachers to take advantage of the possibilities offered to them, pedagogical journals published studies on these works: thus, *Le français aujourd'hui* devoted an issue in March 1988 to "Francophone Literatures," edited by myself and Jean Verrier. It includes articles on Kateb Yacine, Camara Laye, and Birago Diop, as well as suggestions for studying Senghor, Ahmed Sefrioui, Mouloud Feraoun, and Joseph Zobel.

The *Instructions* published in 1995 set the wheels in motion for a renovation of the entire system, based on the notion of discursive mastery, to be acquired through closely linked practices of reading and writing. Progress in skills of argumentation became the major focus. Lists of works disappeared, except in the case of "foundation" texts (the Bible, *The Odyssey, The Aeneid*) and were replaced by generic indications ("a text of critical derision," "a travel narrative," "a nineteenth-

---

The elite track begins with university-level work done in the preparatory classes of the high schools, followed by successful performance on the entrance exam to an *École Normale Supérieure*, where recruiting exams are prepared for, then subsidized doctoral studies undertaken. This track makes it possible for the majority of the students to "escape" from secondary school teaching. The ordinary track begins with university-level work done in a university, followed by doctoral studies undertaken while teaching in a middle or high school. Is one group of students better than the other? The debate is both irresolvable and endless.

or twentieth-century play," and so on), which are more open and thus leave the teacher with greater freedom of choice—presuming, of course, that his/her university training gives him/her the concrete possibility of exercising a choice.

Let me add another word about the secondary level, specifically about high schools. The 1970 reform of the baccalaureate exam eliminated the list of works obligatory for the oral part of the exam, replacing it with a list of authors and texts studied in the course of the year. The written part was composed of a choice among three types of subject: summary, commentary, and literary essay. It was thus entirely possible to include a Francophone work or group of works on the list presented at the oral exam.[4] A look at the lists for the oral shows, unfortunately, that teachers do not take advantage of this possibility, systematically giving priority to works like *Les fleurs du mal, Dom Juan* or *Candide,* ignoring (or ignorant of!) Francophone works. In addition, students did not fail to notice that, in those cases where a Francophone work was included on the list, the examiner rarely chose to ask a question about it!

The situation is a little better in the case of the literature exam for the *Terminale L* class, an exam introduced in 1994 and corresponding (since 2001) to four hours of class per week in the literary track of the final year of high school. The notion here is to round out the cultural knowledge of those students who will go on to literary studies, by having them study important texts taken from a variety of areas of French, Francophone, and foreign literatures. These have included Aimé Césaire's *Discours sur le colonialisme,*[5] his *Cahier d'un retour au pays natal,* and Senghor's *Ethiopiques.*[6]

One cannot say that things have not evolved in French high schools; however, the movement remains very slow. It is as if the weight of the traditional humanities is still very heavy or—and in a sense, this

4. For example, in an article published in *Le français aujourd'hui* 106 (June 1994), "Lire/Écrire en pays créole," teachers of high-school seniors in a school in Martinique, gathered together by Monique Palcy, made up a list of six Caribbean works on the theme of "The City in Caribbean Space": *L'homme au bâton* (Ernest Pépin); *Texaco* (Patrick Chamoiseau); *Le marchand de larmes* (Xavier Orville); *Jacmel au crépuscule* (Jean Métellus); *Cette île qui est la nôtre* (Georges Desportes); and *Cahier d'un retour au pays natal* (Aimé Césaire).

5. This work was supposed to remain on the list for two years but disappeared after only one. The official version: "too difficult." Or perhaps too subversive?

6. The advantage of having this or that author on a list like this is that it immediately brings forth special issues of journals or the publication of little books to accompany it.

amounts to the same thing—as if the training of teachers of French is not sufficient to allow them to take advantage of the possibilities offered by curricula that are, after all, quite open. This invites us to take a look at university-level teaching.

University-level Teaching

Just as it is true that secondary-school teaching is centralized and directed from above by the Ministry of Education and the Inspection Générale, it is equally true that university teaching enjoys great autonomy, at least in the area of determining the content of courses of study. There are of course official documents that define the national degrees (*DEUG, licence,* and *maîtrise*), but only at the level of the number of hours of coursework required. This explains why certain universities have given more importance than others to the teaching of Francophone literatures in the program of coursework required for an undergraduate degree in modern literature. At some universities, Francophone literatures may constitute a discreet optional block of courses, while at others they are included in the set of required courses, in greater or smaller proportion. No general description of the situation exists; even if it did, it would have to be continually updated, since the existence of courses on Francophone literature depends on the teachers in place at a given moment; as soon as someone retires or takes a position somewhere else, the courses he/she was teaching are threatened.

The career of French university professors is subject to two obligations: they must have their scholarship officially recognized and they must find a teaching position that corresponds to their field of specialization.

The recognition of one's scholarship takes place via the following obstacle course. Having defended a thesis (if possible, with highest honors: Très honorable avec les félicitations), scholars must also have it "qualified" by the National Committee of Universities (Comité National des Universités, or CNU). It is not until this qualification has been obtained that they can apply for a vacant position as a professor (Maître de Conférences). The same procedure must be repeated for promotion to the higher rank of full professor (Professeur des Universités): a scholar must be favorably reviewed as a potential director of research and then must request qualification by the CNU. Once the qualification has been obtained, teachers may apply for those advertised vacant positions that correspond to their profile.

Francophone literature specialists are thus faced with a thorny problem: the CNU is separated into two possible "receiving" (i.e., qualifying) divisions, which claim to be friendly to each other but in fact are rivals—the Ninth Division, "French Language and Literature," and the Tenth Division, "General and Comparative Literature."[7] To take a somewhat pessimistic view, one could argue that a Francophone literature specialist will not be very well received by either of these divisions. For the Ninth Division, strictly subdivided by historical period, the Francophone scholar belongs to the twentieth-century specialists, but in fact scholars of Francophone literature constitute a very small proportion of those specialists and are regarded with some condescension by scholars of Proust, Claudel, or René Char. This same scholar will scarcely be better received in the Tenth Division, in the sense that "real" comparatists work on two bodies of work that are clearly culturally *and linguistically* distinct (German Romanticism and French Romanticism, for example). In the case of Francophone writers, the existence of a second language sometimes makes itself clearly known (as in the case of Kourouma, Confiant, or Kateb Yacine, for example), but sometimes this is much less clear.

This difficulty in finding one's true place manifests itself when the moment comes in department meetings to "profile," as they say, a position, that is to say to assign it to an area of specialization. Suppose that there's only one position to be had and that two requests have been put forward: one in seventeenth century and the other in Francophone literature. One may—alas!—safely predict that more often than not, the latter will lose out. To put it bluntly, there are very few positions "profiled" for Francophone literatures and thus very few opportunities for young scholars in the field. It is easy to understand why, in these conditions, so few young doctoral candidates commit to a specialization in Francophone literary studies, why so few tenured professors occupy positions with that title (there are three or four), and why so few are liable to direct, officially, specialized research in the field. When such a rare bird leaves, it can be said—to parody Amadou Hampaté Bâ—that "an entire field dies." Only three universities—Paris IV-La Sorbonne and the universities of the Caribbean and Réunion —continually maintain positions in Francophone literature. It is important to

7. The Ninth Division is much larger than the Tenth: 1038 *professeurs* and *maîtres de conférence* in the former, 218 in the latter. Since a Francophone literature category is not officially recognized, we do not know how many Francophonists belong to one or the other commission.

add, however, that in several French universities, there are little clusters of Francophone specialists (three or four) likely to influence the choices made and thus to perpetuate the teaching of Francophone literature; one could cite Paris XIII-Villetaneuse, Cergy-Pontoise, Montpellier III-Paul Valéry, and Bordeaux III-Michel de Montaigne.

To conclude this analysis of the university level, it is clear how difficult it is to give a numerical status report on the teaching of Francophone literature, due to the great diversity of situations from one university to another. It is also clear, however, that in spite of significant inroads here and there, the teaching of Francophone literatures remains a fragile enterprise and does not reflect the blossoming of these literatures in publication, in literary criticism, and in the media. Students thus generally lack solid training in this area, which explains why those of them who become middle or high school teachers remain so timid when the opportunity arises to take advantage of the possibilities offered by the official curricula.

But we can't simply rely on these reasons, internal to the educational system, to explain the resistance of the teaching profession to the development of Francophone studies. Why is it that the country that gave the Prix Goncourt to René Maran for *Batouala, véritable roman nègre* in 1921, then turned its back on the official recognition of a new literature in French? To answer this question, I shall propose three reasons that seem to me to function within the depths of the French intellectual psyche, no doubt to different degrees, but nonetheless constantly.

HERITAGE: GENIUS AND THE DENIAL OF HISTORY

Francophone Literatures and French Literary Heritage

In France today, there exists among intellectuals a strong faction who regret what they call a "decline" or "decadence" of literary studies. Alain Finkielkraut, Danielle Sallenave, Marc Fumaroli, Jacqueline de Romilly, to cite only the most visible members of this roiling cohort, say that they have realized that French language and literature no longer have the worldwide influence they used to have, that the French themselves no longer know the most basic rules of their language— starting with those of spelling—, and that things are even worse in terms of literature, in the sense that not only are the teachers ignorant but that the Ministry of Education itself advises them to abandon literature in favor of exercises of communication or of pure rhetoric.

To cite an example: the literary essay (*dissertation*) is one of the three questions offered to candidates taking the written portion of the baccalaureate exam (the EAF or Épreuve Anticipée de Français), but the number of candidates who choose this question (which is thought to be risky) has diminished by worrisome proportions, when in fact it is the only question that requires a real knowledge of French literature. What to do? Acting on the situation, the ministry plans to reformulate that part of the exam. There is a mobilization of the noble defenders of the teaching of a traditional, national literature: "The ministry is killing literature." A war of communiqués, petitions, manifestos, name-calling, and all sorts of anathema breaks out. . . . Let's condense the account of the heroic exploits of the war between the reformists and the conservatives and of nearly everyone united against the clumsy minister at the time, Claude Allègre (who ended up a casualty of the affair), and focus our attention on the notion of heritage that is at the heart of these debates.

Literary heritage is traditionally constituted by that body of texts or of authors, knowledge of which is supposed to constitute a basis of collective national identity. It is on this heritage that the definition of an identitarian French culture rests, that is to say in which the French recognize the values that they consider to be theirs. A 1992 survey conducted among middle school teachers asked the question: "Cite ten works that, for you, are part of the national literary heritage." The results included works by approximately fifty authors, 94 percent of whom were French; the top twenty were Molière, Hugo, Flaubert, Racine, Balzac, Baudelaire, Corneille, Zola, Voltaire, Stendhal, La Fontaine, Camus, Montaigne, Rabelais, Proust, Maupassant, Pagnol, Rousseau, Fournier, and Daudet (or Homer). This list includes only four twentieth-century authors, and no Francophone authors at all. The implications are stark. At the same time, to the question "Is the transmission of the national literary heritage one of the primary tasks of middle school teaching?," 57 percent of these teachers answered in the affirmative, because "these are our roots" and 43 percent in the negative, because "we need to give priority to language," "to communication," "to reading," "to methods."[8]

Is the exclusion of Francophone writers attributable only to the fact that they are not well known? Probably not; one might also imagine that they are not perceived as contributors to *French* identity. From a

8. Danièle Manesse, "Quels textes enseigne-t-on au collège aujourd'hui?," *Le français aujourd'hui* 100 (December 1992): 47–55.

completely French perspective, this doesn't seem wrong at first, but it becomes so if one considers that the definition of French identity today must take into account the multicultural reality of the country and of the Francophone world that is closely associated with it. What can be said for sure is that as long as a definition of the national literary heritage based on lists of authors predominates, Francophone authors will be unlikely to be included in curricula. The new curricula recently put in place at all levels of elementary and secondary education seem to suggest that the primary goal of the literature teacher will cease to be defined in terms of national heritage. This is intended, on the one hand, to suggest a more cosmopolitan conception, seeking to impart, by training in deliberative writing, a maximum of social autonomy. On the other hand its goal is to benefit reading, reading in all directions, reading for discovery, for curiosity, or for commentary. If this shift away from a focus on national heritage indeed takes place, then Francophone literatures may benefit from the aura of sympathy and curiosity that surrounds them. But even then, the university-level training of teachers will have to have provided them with the minimum required competence in history and literature.

The Genius of the French Language

It seems to me that another significant stumbling-block to the development of Francophone studies in France is the ideology of the "genius of the French language," which still plays a role in such matters.

Since the late eighteenth century, the myth of the genius of the French language has contaminated all reflections on the subject of literature. When Voltaire wrote at mid-century, in the "Language" article of his *Dictionnaire philosophique,* that "the genius of our language is its *clarity* and *order,*" he situated his assertion in a relatively abstract theoretical debate between logic and language. He found himself, furthermore, immediately contradicted by his contemporary Beauzée, who for his part asserts that "without exception, no language is more prone to *obscurity* than ours."[9] Nevertheless, with Rivarol, these as-

9. Cited by Jacques-Philippe Saint-Gérand, "One of the phrases whose meaning is the most vague and whose usage is the most widespread in the modern idiom is 'the genius of the French language of the nineteenth century (1780–1960) . . . with a little prolongation up to the present day,'" in H. Meschonnic, ed., *Et le génie des langues?* (Saint Denis: Presses Universitaires de Vincennes, 2000), 19. On these debates, see Henri Meschonnic, *De la langue française* (Paris: Hachette, 1997), 356.

sertions left behind the world of abstract ideas and entered into the political domain, having taken on a nationalist tinge: "That which is not clear is not French; that which is not clear is English, Italian, Greek, or Latin."[10] All debate was cut off by reducing the idea of the "genius of a language"—which might be of some interest if the point were to analyze its structural or functional specificity—to that of the genius (understood in the sense of superiority) of a people or a nation. Henceforth, and to this day, people would simply speak of "French genius" to sing the praises of the grandeur of France or to lament the fact that the grandeur is no longer what it was in the good old days when all of Europe spoke French. Very quickly, people came to confuse the genius of writers with the genius of the language. Marcel Proust was already protesting this in 1908: "The only people who defend the French language (like the Army during the Dreyfus Affair) are those who attack it. The idea that there is a French language that exists apart from writers, and that must be protected, is outrageous. Each writer must create his language, just as each violinist must create his 'sound.'"[11]

It seems to me that this confusion is the second factor in the rejection (perhaps unconscious on the part of some) suffered by Francophone writers. How could writers who are not really French express French genius? This is what Maurice Grammont implied in 1908, speaking about French verse: "No significant modification of our verse seems to be called for, and it would be especially difficult to applaud the attempts that have been made, generally by foreigners or people with bad senses of humor, to replace it with a radically different type, without taking into account the genius and the demands of the language."[12] Certainly, when André Breton wrote of Aimé Césaire, "He is a black man who handles the French language as no white man today can,"[13] he seemed to be breaking free of the orthodox view. And yet there is a sort of naïve will to shock the bourgeois by situating the battle within the simplistic black/white opposition; the phrase "*handle* the French language" leads one to suspect an instrumentalist conception of a language *endowed by nature* with an absolute *genius*. In the last analysis, the right

10. *Discours sur l'universalité de la langue française* (1784).
11. Letter to Mme. Strauss, 6 November 1908, in *Correspondance 8*, 276.
12. *Petit traité de versification française* (Paris: Librairie Armand Colin, 1908). The work is still in print. Let us remember that Jean Moréas was of Greek origin and Apollinaire Italian and Polish.
13. "Un grand poète noir," preface to the 1947 Bordas edition of *Cahier d'un retour au pays natal*.

to become a major writer—by fully appropriating the French language, making it a personal idiom—does not seem to be as easily accepted as one might think. No doubt this is because a transhistorical ideology of the supremacy of the language remains very strong in this old country.

The Apoliticism of the Teacher of Literature

When I was in high school in the 1950s, there was a very widely held belief that teachers of literature were not supposed to "be political" and that their function was to awaken the young souls entrusted to their masterful authority to the "beauties" of the literary text. Since then, the vocabulary has evolved a bit, but it is not clear that this esthetic conception of the literary text does not live on to this day. Is it not this idea that allows, for example, people to explain that Céline is a great "stylist" even if his thinking is detestable? This is, in short, a dualistic conception, which separates form and content and tries—with great difficulty—to make the frenzied anti-Semitism of the author of *Voyage au bout de la nuit* palatable.

Francophone writers have no chance of winning this game, because they have too many handicaps working against them. Indeed, the first generation not only conveyed an anticolonialist message that constituted a continual assault on imperial policy and the values on which it prided itself (including the genius of the French language!), but on top of that, their French, "in the service" of an ideology as they said back then, fell short of elegance and French good taste, no matter how hard they tried. Things did not get better with the generations that followed: miscegenation, marooning (*marronnage*), and creolization (*métissage*) as poetic arguments may well be met with favor by certain critics, and novels by Glissant, Chamoiseau, or Kourouma may well win literary prizes (in 1958, 1992, and 2000, respectively), but that does not do much more in terms of having that body of literature included in elementary school, middle school, high school, or university curricula than did the awarding of the *Prix Goncourt* to René Maran's *Batouala* in 1921.

Let's take, as an example of the politically incorrect, the role of sexuality in the novels of Raphaël Confiant and Dany Laferrière. Represented as a driving force of human behavior, analyzed within the highly racialized postcolonial context that predominates in the Caribbean as a sort of social revenge, indifferent to any feminism, while nonetheless refusing to spare men, this depiction of sexuality is perceived by the critics as an element of "writing filled with sunlight" or as a gust of "an off-coast breeze that alternately warms and cools the spirit;"[14] in short, as a pleasant aspect of exoticism but one that does not stand up to the intellectualism and seriousness of the books published by the Éditions de Minuit.[15]

Perhaps it is safer for Western critics to represent these writers as entertainers and clowns than to invite Western culture to look at itself in certain mirrors, including that of sexuality. The outcry in France that greeted Michel Houellebecq's latest work, *Plateforme,* in which he ferociously and forcefully denounces sexual tourism, clearly shows that this culture is no better prepared to look at its recent history (its anti-Semitic racism, its anti-Arab racism) than at its present.

*   *   *   *   *

That an analysis of the status of the teaching of Francophone literatures in France today should end on a political note will come as no surprise, since language and literature define themselves in every era through political debate. Aside from idealistic esthetic positions, there is in fact no universal definition of literature that holds true, in and of itself, for all cultures, in all eras. Language and its representation, literature and its representation, come together poetically to produce the idiom of their time. Francophone literatures are not yet perceived in France as an idiom of the French, hence the deaf resistance to integrating them fully into the curricula of schools and universities. A sign of the timidity of French culture? It would not be the first time the term has been used.

—Translated by Christopher Rivers

14. These expressions come from the pen of critic André Brincourt in *Le Figaro,* 4 November 1994, in reference to Raphaël Confiant's *Allée des soupirs.*

15. Daniel-Henri Pageaux compares Raphaël Confiant to Frédéric Dard, alias San Antonio, and presents him as the champion of a "virulent anti-intellectualism, attacking the schools and the classics while extolling the warm conviviality of the world of gambling and sex." See "Raphaël Confiant ou la traversée paradoxale d'une décennie," *Portulan* (February 1996): 35–58.

JEAN JONASSAINT

Literatures in the
Francophone Caribbean[1]

In Barthesian terms, my initial question could be: What is literature in the Francophone Caribbean World? For, as Roland Barthes argued, thinking the teaching of literature is at the same time defining literature, an object that exists only as a teaching matter.[2] And so, in order to answer this question, we need to ask others: What governs the establishment of the curriculum and the choice of literary textbooks at secondary and university levels? What governs the content of examination questions and the subjects of theses or dissertations in literature in Caribbean universities? To complicate matters, this inquiry must also take into account the different political statuses of both main parts of the Francophone Caribbean complex and their inequalities of development at all levels.

In this Caribbean space already divided by its geography and history, there is a fundamental difference between the Haitian Republic and

1. This article is a shorter English version of a study to be published in French on the status of Francophone literatures in the Caribbean. For a general understanding of the French and Haitian School and University systems see: "The French Higher Education System": *http://www.egide.asso.fr/uk/comprendre/home.htm*; "Le système éducatif français": *http://www.education.gouv.fr/syst/default.htm*; Antoine Levy, *Rapport sur l'éducation en Haïti (soumis au Bureau International de l'Éducation)* (Port-au-Prince: Ministère de l'Éducation Nationale de la Jeunesse et des Sports, 1996); available from *http://www.ibe.unesco.org/International/Databanks/Dossiers/rhaiti.htm*; Ruth J. Simmons, *Haiti: A Study of the Educational System of Haiti and a Guide to the Academic Placement of Students in Educational Institutions of the United States* (Washington, D.C.: International Education Activities Group of the American Association of Collegiate Registrars and Admissions Officers, 1985); Pierre Vernet, "La réforme éducative en Haïti. Philosophie, objectifs, stratégies et contenus," *Études créoles* 7/1–2 (1984): 142–63.

2. See Roland Barthes, "Réflexions sur un manuel," in *L'enseignement de la littérature (entretiens du Centre culturel de Cerisy-la-Salle, 22 au 29 juillet 1969)*, ed. Serge Doubrovsky and Tzvetan Todorov (Paris: Plon, 1971), 170–77.

YFS 103, *French and Francophone*, ed. Farid Laroussi and Christopher L. Miller,
© 2003 by Yale University.

Martinique and Guadeloupe, between the *dependent* French Antilles and *independent* Haïti (to borrow Maryse Condé's distinction in *La parole des femmes*[3]), despite the so-called common Creole languages, and their common belonging to the sphere of French influence. Guadeloupeans and Martinicans are French citizens who benefit entirely from the French socioeconomic environment—their per capita GDP is closer to that of the EEC than to that of Haitians. Furthermore, despite the obvious shortcomings of the French Antillean school system that have so often been denounced, the literacy rate in the French Antilles is much higher than in Haiti (90 percent of Martinicans and Guadelopeans can read and write, compared to 45 percent of the Haitian population).[4]

Such differences in the socioeconomic profile of these populations are not without effect on their perception and insertion in the world. There is even a saying—not so far from the truth—that Guadeloupeans and Martinicans are today among the few French citizens who have been 100 percent French for more than 150 years. In contrast, Haitians, even if they are partly Francophone, are not French, have never been French, and, *de jure* or *de facto*, do not benefit from their common belonging to the "Francophone sphere."

TOWARD A DELIMITATION OF LITERARY FIELDS IN THE CARIBBEAN

This set of historical and structural differences implies differences in the delimitation or definition of the Haitian and the French Antillean literary corpuses. In fact, the ideological postulates or presuppositions that rule the delimitation and definition of those literatures are quite opposed, the ethnic closure of the one contrasting with the racial crossing of the other.

For Haitians, their literature begins with independence in 1804, and consists of Haitian works, that is, those of the former Black slaves and their descendents who gained freedom and citizenship after their victory against Napoleon's Army. This basic postulate is clearly stated in the introduction to the first Haitian literary history by Vaval, subtitled "*l'âme noire*," or "the black soul": "this volume is the history of the literature of Black Africans uprooted to Saint-Domingue, as they be-

3. Maryse Condé, *La parole des femmes. Essai sur des romancières des Antilles de langue français* (Paris: L'Harmattan, 1979).
4. See CIA, *The World Factbook 2001* (http://www.cia.gov/cia/publications/factbook/).

come conscious of their humanity."[5] This postulate is restated less than thirty years later by Ghislain Gouraige, who clearly asserts the historical limits of his work in his title, *Histoire de la littérature haïtienne (de l'Indépendance à nos jours)* (The History of Haitian Literature [from Independence to Today]). One year later, in the introduction to their *Manuel illustré d'histoire de la littérature haïtienne*, even if they recognize that some literary works were inspired by the local customs of Saint-Domingue before the Haitian Revolution, Frères de l'Instruction Chrétienne and Pompilus think: "Nevertheless, Haitian Literature was really born with Liberty in 1804."[6]

Criticism in Martinique and Guadeloupe has seen colonial literature as an integral part of the local corpus, a corpus that includes the production of two groups that are ethnically or racially identified: "Whites" and "Blacks." Moreover, the history of this literature is articulated around one very important turning point, the abolition of slavery in the French Antilles in 1848, which allowed the Black and Mulatto populations to progressively gain access to citizenship and education, and to total participation in the life of their land. On this point, Roger Toumson's argument on the scope of Afro-Antillean literature is very explicit:

> For a precise definition of Afro-Antillean literature in French (*stricto sensu*), it is suitable . . . to conceive of Antillean literature in French (*largo sensu*) as a dual discursive structure: its whole being is subdivided in two subsets. The Creole writers' production (White literature of the eighteenth, nineteenth, and twentieth centuries) constitutes the first part of its double *ensemble;* the production of the Colored and Black writers (nineteenth and twentieth centuries) is the second part of this functional couple. Within these subsets defined as such, it is advisable as well to detect the mechanism of influences exerted by the literary models given by French literature, phase after phase, in its entire duration. We have to examine the double determination mechanism sustained by Afro-Antillean literature, on the one hand, because of the complementary relation that it maintains with White Creole literature, and, on the other hand, because of the influence exerted by French metropolitan literature in a continuous manner.[7]

5. Duraciné Vaval, *Histoire de la littérature haïtienne ou "l'âme noire"* (Port-au-Prince: 1933), 7.

6. Frères de l'Instruction Chrétienne and Pradel Pompilus, *Manuel illustré d'histoire de la littérature haïtienne* (Port-au-Prince: Éditions H. Deschamps, 1961), 7.

7. Roger Toumson, *La transgression des couleurs. Littérature et langage es Antilles XVIIIᵉ. XIXᵉ et XXᵉ siècles*, vol. 1 (Paris: Éditions Caribéennes, 1989), 7–8.

The principle of complementarity and inclusion between White and Black literature, French and French Antillean literature that Toumson advocates for the early period of this literary history is expanded upon by Patrick Chamoiseau and Raphael Confiant for the late period in their reading of the Caribbeanness (*antillanité*) or creoleness (*créolité*) of the works of the White Creole Antillean Saint-John Perse (1887–1975) and the French metropolitan Salvat Etchart (1932–1985), whom they considered as Antillean writers even though the former had left his native Guadeloupe as a child, and the latter lived in Martinique for only about ten years.[8] Thus, French Antillean literary history, like its Québécois counterpart, includes in its body the colonial text which is also French literature from overseas, that is, texts written by French nationals living outside the Hexagon. Of course, this colonial corpus intersects with the very notion of Francophone literature, but does not overlap it. Moreover, for the contemporary period, those literatures also include texts by French metropolitans who have lived in the New World, like the famous *Maria Chapdelaine* by Louis Hémon (1916) in the Québécois corpus. If those French Antillean or Québécois literatures that integrate a part of the French corpus are "Francophone," the notion of Francophone literature should not be defined simply as literature written in French outside of France. One must highlight the ambiguity of the notions of French and Francophone literature in the French Antilles context, since these literatures intersect and are, to some extent, part of one another. In this sense, the introduction of the French Caribbean production in the French Antillean curriculum could always be read in the light of a French policy of decentralization or regionalization rather than a policy of opening onto the Francophone world. In contrast, in Haiti, the dynamic is quite different. French and Haitian literatures are two distinct corpuses, despite the influence of French metropolitan literature on Haitian writers.

ON THE TEACHING OF LITERATURES

Both historically and theoretically, Haitians exclusively hold all power within their territory, whereas the Antilles are ruled by French or European laws, with, beginning in the 1980s, some delegation of powers that allows for a certain administrative autonomy in local and regional

8. Patrick Chamoiseau and Raphaël Confiant, *Lettres créoles. Tracées antillaises et continentales de la littérature 1635–1975* (Paris: Hatier, 1991), 160–70.

decision-making. However, the regional decision-making power of French Antilleans in the field of education, particularly following bulletin n° 82–261 of 21 June 1982 issued by the Department of National Education, has its *de facto* limitations, mainly caused by the state examinations and competitions at the end of every important cycle of training, particularly those concerning teacher certification, the *capès* and the *agrégation*.[9]

Indeed, although the different academies decide upon the examination questions for the *Baccalauréat* (secondary school diploma) with a concern for regional flexibility and adaptability, this is far from the case for the *capès* and *agrégation,* where there is a single state examination, and the same jury for all candidates. Therefore, it is clear that a marked preference for canonical metropolitan French literature overdetermines the choice of examination topics, and even the questions in the field of comparative literature leave no room for Francophone literatures or writers from outside of Europe, or even outside of France. These examination topics, more than any other source, reveal the true state of literary studies in Martinique and Guadeloupe, which is almost entirely similar to the situation in the Hexagon, particularly in the field of teacher training. Indeed, the examination questions in the Académie des Antilles et de la Guyane are in no way different from those of other academies in the French Republic, and mirror more or less the questions of the *capès* and *agrégation* examinations.[10] The obvious reason for this is that professors who have been trained in a purely French literary tradition do not make up examination questions in areas in which they have no specific training, or which they even look down upon; such subjects were rarely, if ever, part of their own curriculum. Of course, a few courses are occasionally offered on a few well-known Caribbean writers such as Césaire, Condé, Glissant, Roumain, Schwartz-Bart, or Zobel. And although there is a graduate program in Creole studies at the Université des Antilles et de la Guyane (U.A.G.),

9. See: *Les annales de l'agrégation de lettres classiques et de grammaire: 1983–1999* (Paris: H. Champion, 1999); *Les annales de l'agrégation de lettres modernes: 1970–1999* (Paris: H. Champion, 1999); *Les annales du CAPES de lettres modernes et de lettres classiques: 1976–1999* (Paris: H. Champion, 1999).

10. See for example: Sylvie Azérad, *Français L, Es, S: corrigés* (Paris: Hatier, 1996); *Français L, Es, S: corrigés* (Paris: Hatier, 1997); *Français L, Es, S: corrigés* [Annabac 1999] (Paris: Hatier, 1998); *Français L, Es, S: corrigés* (Paris: Hatier, 1999); *Français L, Es, S: corrigés* (Paris: Hatier, 2000); Danielle Girard, "Liste des textes de commentaires littéraires" (1996–2000): *http://www.ac-rouen.fr/pedagogie/equipes/lettres/comment/incipit2.html.*

there is no program in Francophone Caribbean literature, nor in Caribbean or Francophone literature in general.

In Haiti, however, Haitian literature in French has been officially included in secondary school curricula since 1959, following the bulletin of 26 October 1959 issued by the Ministry of National Education. The latter also approved a textbook in 1961 to sustain the teaching of this subject, which is a compulsory examination subject for Baccalauréat candidates in all sections. Also, the Haitian curriculum, unlike the French Antillean one, reserves an equally important place for French and Caribbean literature, that is, Haitian literature from 1804 until the 1960s. According to Pompilus,[11] the teaching of Haitian literature at the Université d'État d'Haïti dates back to 1951. This field of study is "one of the great originalities of the École Normale Supérieure," and has spread to several other graduate schools, thus becoming one of the most developed fields of study of Haitian higher education. This conclusion has been confirmed by a rapid analysis of the list of theses presented to the École Normale Supérieure from 1950 to 1977, compiled by Wilfried Bernard.[12] Hence, Pompilus is probably right to claim that, at the École Normale Supérieure, "[students] almost exclusively tend to favor questions concerning [Haiti]."

To some extent, researchers and students at the U.A.G. have also shared a similar interest in indigenous studies since the university was created in 1982.[13] One notable distinction, however, is that whatever (independent) Haitians exclusively articulate in national terms, (non-independent) French Antillean researchers and students express in regional terms. This explains why, during the period Bernard studies, no thesis from the Université d'État d'Haïti was devoted, partially or entirely, to a writer from Martinique or Guadeloupe. Indeed, although some theses treat French or even Latin American writers, none has ever been written on Césaire, the first literature professor in 1944 at the "Cours Normaux Supérieurs for the training and enhancement of sec-

11. Pradel Pompilus, *Au service de l'enseignement national et de la jeunesse* (Port-au-Prince: Éditions Pegasus, 1996), 148–49, 165.

12. Wilfrid Bernard, "Travaux de recherches à l'Université d'État d'Haïti," *Conjonction* 136/137 (1978): 145–155.

13. See, for example, Université des Antilles et de la Guyane, "Présentation de la stratégie internationale de l'UAG": *http://www.univ-ag.fr/uag/f—inter.htm;* "Programmes internationaux menés par l'université": *http://www.univ-ag.fr/uag/bri/prog.htm;* "La recherche à Schoelcher": *http://www.martinique.univ-ag.fr/Recherch.html.*

ondary school professors" (Pompilus, 147), and whose teaching at the time, according to René Depestre,[14] deeply influenced his generation. Haitians, in fact, consider the regional or indigenous reality as merely national (Haitian).

This quite reductive conception of the literary field becomes evident on analyzing the indexes of writers included in textbooks on Haitian literature by Frères de l'Instruction Chrétienne and Pompilus as well as by Gouraige.[15] Although Gouraige's field of reference is larger than that of Frères de l'Instruction Chrétienne and Pompilus, he nevertheless remains constrained by a certain classicism, and particularly by the notion that Francophone literatures are primarily indebted to European forms and themes.

Of course, such a discourse clearly reflects the state of knowledge and literary preoccupations of the 1950s and 1960s, but this phenomenon also points to the bias of the Haitian intelligentsia who have taken but little interest in the French Antilles. At the U.A.G. in contrast, not only is Haitian literature taught, but Haitian works, like those of Frankétienne, have been included in doctoral research, namely in Confiant's 1997 dissertation on Creolophone writing.[16] The difference is further apparent when analyzing Jack Corzani's textbook, which systematically reads contemporary literature from Martinique, Guadeloupe, and Guyane in relation to both Haitian or Caribbean literatures and African literatures, even though the principal corpus for comparison remains French canonical literature.[17] It is important, however, to bear in mind that there is no longer a consensus in regard to this global conception of French Caribbean space. As is apparent from issues 121–122 of *Présence africaine* (1982) on "Antilles-Guyane," although Haiti does not necessarily disappear, it is increasingly marginalized, as in the collective volume *Écrire la "parole de nuit." La nouvelle littérature antillaise* (1994).

14. Phone conversation of 27 October 2001.

15. Frères de l'Instruction Chrétienne and Pradel Pompilus, 601–8; Ghislain Gouraige, *Histoire de la littérature haïtienne. De l'Indépendance à nos jours* (Port-au-Prince: Imprimerie Théodore, 1960), 497–507.

16. Confiant, *Kreyol pale, kreyol matje . . . analyse des significations attachées aux aspects littéraires, linguistiques et socio-historiques de l'écrit créolophone entre 1750 et 1995 aux petites Antilles, en Guyane et an Haïti* (Fort de France: Université des Antilles et de la Guyane, 1997).

17. See: Jack Corzani, *La littérature des Antilles-Guyane françaises* (Fort-de-France: Désormeaux 1978), 6 volumes.

TOWARD A PRESENT AND FUTURE INVENTORY
OF CARIBBEAN LITERATURE

Until today, despite a variety of reforms in France as well as in Haiti, the French Letters programs in French Antillean and Haitian secondary schools are more or less, with a few exceptions in Haiti, the same as those of French secondary schools. Students use the same French literature textbooks, and classical French literature is at the core of all literary training and literary thought, regardless of whether the object of the study is a Caribbean or Haitian text. Moreover, in Martinique and Guadeloupe, Francophone literature in the Caribbean—whether by Caribbean writers or not—is not included in the examination questions of State competitions; and in Haiti only Haitian literature is a topic of examination. At the university level, Francophone literatures are not better served. The Modern Letters program at the U.A.G. includes some classes on Francophone literatures, but not as many as at some other French universities, such as Paris Nord, which has a Diplôme d'études approfondies (DEA) in Francophone literatures. In Haiti, the only Francophone literature in the curriculum is Haitian literature. Hence, these Caribbean examples seem to indicate that the notion of Francophone literature as a transnational corpus is a concept of (and for) spaces that are not strictly speaking Francophone (such as, for example, the United States). In Francophone countries per se, Francophone literature is the national literature (Haiti), a regional literature (French Antilles), and a pan-regional or a pan-ethnic literature (Africa). In the Caribbean, Francophone literature is therefore either a (national) variety of Francophone Caribbean literatures in Haiti, or a (regional) variety of French literature in the DOM.

One cannot predict the future, but it would seem that the new French program, with its emphasis on literary genre rather than on historical periods, and with its "six objects of study," one of which is "Francophone literatures," should theoretically favor the teaching of Francophone literatures, by privileging the freedom of the instructor to choose for his or her class works closer to the students, rather than any "dogmatic canonical list." But this may not occur.[18] Indeed, due to the recent pressures that the new *capès* in Creole[19] is putting on the entire

18. For an authoritative synthesis of the new program of French and its challenges, see Alain Viala, "Les nouveaux programmes de lycée et leurs enjeux," *http://www. eduscol.eucation/fr/DOO11/viala-nov00html*; and Alain Boissinot, "Où en est l'enseignement du français?," *Le débat* 110 (May–August 2000).
19. See: CAPES de créole/KAPES Kréyol: *http://kapeskreol.online.fr*.

Caribbean education system, "Creole" languages and literatures may be gaining popularity at the expense of Francophone literatures. The latter are isolated within the branches of general or comparative literatures, and have no weight in departments and on State examinations.

France's decision (in 2001) to make Creole an official academic language may have an even greater impact on Haiti, where this Haitian language has already been, at least theoretically, included in the curriculum (as a target and tool language) at all levels of the education system, following Bernard's 1982 reform. Indeed, France's recognition of the Creole language will bring grist to the mill of those who would partly or totally remove French literature from the Haitian curriculum, for French-language learning must receive more and more focus, and, in the short or long term, the curriculum must include "Creole literature." However, there are no signs that Francophone literature other than Haitian will be more, if at all, present. Because the confusion between native, learning, and academic languages carries the potential danger of tending toward demagogy, Haitian literature in French may even progressively disappear from secondary school curricula, both under the internal pressure of Creolophone writers and editors who insist on having recognition in the program, and under the external pressure of the Haitian Diaspora in the United States. These Haitians are increasingly Americanized, and no longer consider French as a privileged language of communication. The latter have, in fact, been publishing more and more frequently and successfully in English and less in French.[20]

This evolution illustrates a historical tendency toward indigenization or autonomy of emerging nations, of which good examples can be found in the European Renaissances. The French language and its literature in the Caribbean may well become another kind of *Latin* in the twenty-second century. But, whatever the outcome, the Francophone literature that will—or could—be taught will be more or less exclusively Caribbean or Black African, but it will also be increasingly marginalized under the pressure of nativisms named "Caribbeanness," (*antillantié*), "creoleness" (*créolité*), or "Haitianness" (*haïtianité*).

20. See: Jean Jonassaint, "Les productions littéraires haïtiennes aux États-Unis (1948–1986)," *Journal of Haitian Studies* 5/6 (1999–2000): 4–19.

AMADOU KONÉ

Teaching Francophone Literature: Remarks from Two Continents

My comments here arise largely from my personal experience as a former student at the Université d'Abidjan and, more importantly, as a
professor, first in Côte d'Ivoire at the same university, and subsequently in the United States. Having found myself in these various situations, I have had the opportunity to observe first-hand the ways in
which the teaching of so-called "Francophone" literature is oriented in
each of these contexts. Of course, these remarks extend beyond mere
observation, for the situations I am describing are caught within the
historical context of Africa as it has developed from French colonization to the present day.

Following independence, it was quickly understood that the links
between the African and French school systems were to remain rigid
and constraining. Abdou Moumouni explains that "the desire of
African governments to see the awarding of degrees identical to French
degrees necessarily imposes 'servitudes' as far as curricula are concerned."[1] He thus poses the crucial question of the *équivalence* (that
is, the curricular congruency and therefore the transferability) of
African and French degrees. This problem, among others, determined
the organization of African educational institutions and their content,
that is, their curricula. For example, the Centre d'Enseignement
Supérieur d'Abidjan, which was established in 1958, and which rapidly
transformed itself into a university, remained until the 1970s a French
university, or had at least quite faithfully copied the structures of
French universities.

When I began there as a student in the seventies, the department of
Modern Literature (meaning French literature) at Abidjan differed very

1. Abdou Moumouni, *L'éducation en Afrique* (Paris: F. Maspéro, 1964), 141.

YFS 103, *French and Francophone,* ed. Farid Laroussi and Christopher L. Miller,
© 2003 by Yale University.

little from its counterparts in France. French literature from the Middle Ages to the twentieth century was taught by specialists in each century. Some rare French and African professors attempted, with great difficulty, to introduce African literature into the curriculum. In the final year, there was a course offered on the African novel alongside courses on Malraux, the Surrealists, and Zola. The course on the African novel was a marginal track within the Certificat de Licence L. Those students who so desired could select the C1 certificate in African Studies, which included one course each in African anthropology, history, and linguistics. At that time, therefore, the *licence* in Modern Literature was composed of the L certificate (French literature plus one course on the African novel), the C1 (African Studies, linguistics, grammar, and so on), and a certificate of proficiency in Latin. This Latin certificate was mandatory for the Ivorian *licence* in Modern Literature to be equivalent to the French *licence*. And this equivalence was necessary for those students such as myself who intended to pursue studies in French universities at levels of instruction not offered at our university: Masters, Diplôme d'études approfondies, and Doctorate.

The introduction of African literature into the curriculum was a difficult process. Indeed, the majority of professors of French literature, all of whom were French citizens, sent abroad by France as part of French foreign aid (*coopération technique et culturelle*), would claim that African literature was not literature and that it was absurd to teach it at the university alongside French authors. Moreover, a debate concerning the very concept of literature was raging. The African professors as well as a few of the French professors insisted on the historical context and social function of literature, while the majority of the French professors emphasized literature's aesthetic aspect as well as its structural play. In addition to the controversy surrounding African literature, there was a debate concerning the most appropriate critical approach for the teaching of this literature.[2] These debates, often muddled, often linked to ideological conflicts and occasionally to conflicts between personalities, nevertheless had the advantage of raising consciousness among us students of the ambiguous predicament of so-called African literature, and of opening us up to a wider contemplation of literature and criticism. For all intents and purposes, however,

2. On this subject, see Barhélémy Kotchy-Nguessan, "Pourquoi la sociocritique?" *Propos sur la littérature négro-africaine,* ed. Christophe Dailly and Barhélémy Kotchy-Nguessan, (Abidjan: CEDA, 1984), 173–184.

African literature remained a marginalized subject lacking recognition from the French cultural establishment and French universities and sometimes even in Africa from skeptical Africans, themselves unconvinced of the value of their own literature.

Upon my return to Abidjan in 1977, after having finished my studies in France, I found that the Université d'Abidjan had become the Université Nationale de Côte d'Ivoire. The change of name did not, perhaps, bear any real relation to an actual change in status. For the question of transferability and the constraints involved in this umbilical relationship still remained. However, with the recruitment of new professors specializing in African literature and the departure of the most conservative French professors, the place for the teaching of African literature had been substantially expanded. Although instruction in French literature by century, in comparative literature, and in African literature remained within the same fundamental structure, a significant degree of balance had been attained. There was a notable change in the status of African literature. It became quite well represented in the curriculum, and henceforth was taught in each of the three years of the *licence*. It was taught by genre: the novel in the first year, theater in the second year, poetry and oral literature in the final year for the D and C1 certificates. Moreover, the teaching of comparative literature, which was rapidly expanding, allowed for the inclusion of African literature within its corpus. Such a situation was possible because now the expertise was available.

One must never lose sight of the problem of degree equivalence. For, even with the aforementioned progress, the Department of Modern Literature remained a Department of French. And in the best of cases, one took half of one's coursework in French literature and the other half in African literature. There was a tacit agreement that French literature would not be neglected.

At the same time, the long debate on oral literature seemed to have arrived at a resolution. The movement that was fighting for the recognition of oral literature seemed to be triumphant in several African universities.[3] The Groupe de Recherches sur les Traditions Orales (GRTO) was established in Abidjan, but this institute was especially concerned with research, namely collection, classification, and translation. It was not concerned with teaching. In fact, this recognition of the funda-

---

3. As Lilyan Kesteloot observes, efforts toward the study of oral traditions took place in Dakar, Yaoundé, and Niamey. *Research in African Literatures* 24/2 (1993).

mental importance of oral literature does not actually seem to have been exploited as it should have been. This literature, existing first and foremost in an African language, should have, at a basic level, complemented instruction in written literature and have led to the introduction of African languages into the university. But no such pedagogy was developed. And as Karim Traoré remarked in a 2000 essay: "Despite the improvement in the curriculum of literary studies and the existence of the various institutes that perform the important work of archiving, we have no choice but to observe that oral literature has not yet been bestowed with the official honors that would allow it to establish itself as a university discipline in its own right."[4]

During the fifteen years I taught at the Université Nationale de Côte d'Ivoire in Abidjan, the situation did not develop in any significant way. The progressive shift from the traditional curriculum to the *Unités de Valeur* (UV) has perhaps allowed for the offering of more courses in African literature. However, at the level of the UV required for the degrees, one comes back to the same predicament, that is, instruction that is disparate and that does not determine the principal orientation of the department.

Since my departure in 1992, the university has been reorganized. As in France, it is no longer a question of *facultés* but rather of *Unités de Formation et de Recherche* (UFR). The names have changed, but the content has remained fundamentally the same. From the point of view of the teaching of literature, nothing has changed. In the UFR of Languages, Literature, and Civilization, one finds the Department of Modern Literature in the same state as before. There remains the constant concern of maintaining a balance between African literature and French literature. The rules governing the equivalence of degrees have not changed either. According to information received from Abidjan, the diplomas awarded in Abidjan are, in principal, equivalent to French degrees and Ivorian students manage to enroll in doctoral programs in France after having obtained the DEA in Abidjan.

What is there to say about the teaching of "Francophone literature" in Africa and, more specifically, in Côte d'Ivoire? A problem still exists, itself inscribed within the larger and more complex problem of the relationship between the French language and African languages, between African culture and French culture, between the overall educational system in African countries and their relationship with the

4. Karim Traoré, *Le jeu et le sérieux* (Cologne: Koppe, 2000), 111.

French educational system. African states have not reconsidered their educational systems since independence, just as they have not reconsidered their cultural politics.[5] Have they not had the political will to do so? The financial means to put in place structures that might have allowed for the implementation of true reforms? Or were they prevented from doing so by the constraints imposed by the former colonial power? Perhaps all of these hypotheses are relevant. The system of equivalence I have described is a powerful coercive tool. It is an artifice that allows France to impose its own system, its own literature, and its own culture. African professors, in cooperation with a few French professors, have had to fight continuously against a system that is fundamentally opposed to a literature that appeared minor in its written form in the French language and that was not even recognized as literature in its oral form.

More than forty years after independence, the French model still prevails. This is, perhaps, also the goal of *Francophonie* in general: to impose a system that is not only linguistic (can it remain purely linguistic?), but that also, little by little, erases the culture of the countries that use French as a language of business and of creativity. For how will we ever escape from this situation if we do not create departments of *African* literature in which African literature would be *central*, thus putting an end to the burdensome domination of French literature? This would allow African literature to be taught in African languages as well as in European languages, and would also assist in the exploration of theoretical fields such as concepts of literature and literary criticism, thereby enriching the universal field of literature. To consider African literature as central and not as a peripheral element, to reflect and discover appropriate critical approaches and a new pedagogy inspired by the very nature of this literature: these seem to me to be the main scholarly objectives in an eventual African literature department. French literature would no longer be the suffocating, encumbering godfather. At the moment, there are no African literature departments except in Yaoundé, in Cameroon; the existence of that program alone is already a huge step. Does this department manage to take advantage of

5. Actually, Guinea and Mali attempted to implement reforms of their respective educational systems following independence. The reorganization that took place in Guinea was both the most daring and the one that introduced African languages into the schools. The failure of this experiment is, of course, due to a complex political context as well as to the lack of the material resources necessary to its implementation. See the analysis of these reforms in Moumouni, 383–88.

the freedom of its solitary status? That is another question, as the Cameroonians are, like all Francophone Africans, subject to the problem of equivalence and that of political *Francophonie.*

Up to this point, for various reasons, I have barely used the word *Francophonie,* the definitions of which seem to me quite vague.[6] In Africa, *Francophonie* refers more to a political entity than to literature. In truth, it is here in the US that I have progressively come to think of the teaching of African literature in French as "Francophone" teaching or as falling under the banner of Francophone studies. Two elements seem important to mention concerning the emergence of this field in American universities. First, this addition to the curriculum came into existence under pressure from students in the early 1960s.[7] It was not without subsequent opposition, occasionally vehement. Christopher Miller has described the violence with which certain university authorities rose up against African literary studies, pleading that the field was a danger to Western studies.[8] This battle seems to have been a rearguard action, for the study continued to prosper. Second, as I have described elsewhere, for the very reason of its coming to America through the structures of *Francophonie,* African literature has been confronted with the same problems as in Africa.[9] Since French departments are organized here following the model of Modern Literature departments in France and in Africa, there is the same problem of the integration of African literature into the programs. While French literature is covered century by century with a course on each, a single survey course on African literature is thought to be sufficient. This literature is underrepresented, suffocated as it is within French departments. Francophone literature, which includes African literature, also encompasses the literatures of Quebec, Belgium, Asia, the Caribbean, and so on. Each

6. For example, reading *Littérature et Francophonie,* published by the Commissariat Général de la Langue Française, leaves one rather perplexed. In the final analysis, one wonders whether *Francophonie* is not a politico-cultural association that, on the surface, is somewhat of a hodgepodge while being an instrument of propagation for French language and culture underneath. See Arlette Chemain-Dégrange, ed., *Littérature et Francophonie* (Nice: CRDP/Commissariat Général de la Langue Française, 1989).

7. Jacqueline Leiner recounts briefly the upsurge of student interest in this subject in "Une expérience entre trois continents et trois cultures," in Chemain-Dégrange, 59–66.

8. See Christopher L. Miller, "Literary Studies and African Literature: The Challenge of Intercultural Literacy," *Africa and the Disciplines,* ed. Robert H. Bates, V. Y. Mudimbe, and John O'Barr (Chicago: University of Chicago Press, 1993), 213–31.

9. See my article "Enseigner la littérature africaine de langue française dans les universités américaines. Notes à partir d'une expérience en cours," *Tangence* 49 (1995): 23–31.

of these literatures take up a minute fraction of the twentieth century, which they are all supposed to share with twentieth-century French literature. There is, perhaps, more exposure at the graduate level, where a regular seminar is given to students who have already chosen a specialty. Yet there as well, considering the limited number of seminars that can be offered each semester, African literature is kept to a strict minimum, for departments make sure that such teaching is not offered to the detriment of French literature, which is, justifiably, the most important subject in a French department. Overall, the conditions under which African literature is presented in French departments lead to quite a superficial type of instruction. This gives a narrow perspective on the literature, which in turn explains the dangerous belief that teaching it is a kind of do-it-yourself pursuit in which anybody can engage. My own experience permits me to say that, too often, professors specializing in another field, having read one or two African novels and a few articles on Orientalism and postcolonialism, declare themselves Francophone literature specialists.

If we examine the issues carefully, the teaching of Francophone literature in American universities poses more complex problems. These problems are related to the conceptual basis of the curriculum within universities, to the nature of the discipline and to the level of knowledge that the students have of Africa, its history, and its culture. All the reports of true specialists in the teaching of Francophone literature in the US emphasize the numerous precautions one must initially take in order to try to achieve one's objective, namely, to make a public with scant knowledge of Africa understand this literature.[10] For reading is also an intertextual process on multiple levels. It is the process of envisioning the relationships between the text, on the one hand, and on the other, history, culture, literary genre, and the literary tradition of a country or a region. Yet we must recognize that American students have, in general, limited knowledge of Africa. Teaching so-called Francophone literature in the US therefore requires inventing strategies which are not the business of an amateur.

---

10. I would especially recommend Eric Sellin's account of the ways in which he undertook teaching Chinua Achebe's novel *Things Fall Apart*. Eric Sellin, "Teaching *Things Fall Apart* in the Humanities Core Course," *Approaches to Teaching Achebe's* Things Fall Apart, ed. Bernth Lindfors (New York: Modern Language Association of America, 1991), 118–22. One might call to my attention that this is an Anglophone African novel. But at this level, this observation does not seem pertinent, for the obstacles mentioned are the same as those encountered in teaching Francophone texts.

As far as Côte d'Ivoire and Africa in general are concerned, it is definitely time to look again at the structures, to rethink literature starting from African literature as a center, which, of course, implies rethinking the question of culture in a comprehensive manner and the question of *Francophonie* not only in relation to language, but also in relation to African culture in general.

—Translated by J. Ryan Poynter

JOSIAS SEMUJANGA

The Fortunes and Misfortunes of Teaching Francophone Literatures in Canada

In bilingual Canada, there is a longstanding tradition of teaching French language and literature. In most if not all Canadian universities, a department of French Studies can be found in which French language and French literature undoubtedly dominate. It is a tradition that on the whole is as old as the universities themselves.

Initiated in the early 1970s, the teaching of Francophone literatures in Canada reached its apex during the 1990s. In order to fully analyze this development, a study was made based on a survey of French departmental websites throughout Canada. The resulting information showed the places where teaching and research are conducted in Francophone literatures, the levels at which they are introduced, and the forms and modalities that characterize the different programs reviewed. The survey was divided into two parts. While the first sought information about the teaching of Francophone literatures—In what format was the teaching being done? What place was given to it in the departmental curriculum?—the second concentrated on research: Was there at least one specialist among the teaching faculty whose research involved a sector of Francophone literature? The results obtained show that Francophone literature remains a marginalized discipline in the teaching program of literary studies in Canada in general and in Quebec in particular.[1] In what follows, I first give a brief history of the teaching of Francophone literatures in Canadian and Quebecois universities, and then summarize the developments of the last thirty years and emphasize present trends. Furthermore, for each of these time periods, I compare the status of Francophone literatures in Quebecois universities to that of their situation in Canadian universities as a whole.

1. Josias Semujanga, "Liminaire," *Tangence* 49 (1995): 5–8.

YFS 103, *French and Francophone*, ed. Farid Laroussi and Christopher L. Miller, © 2003 by Yale University.

THE EVOLUTION OF QUEBECOIS LITERATURE
TOWARD A NATIONAL LITERATURE

The term "Quebecois literature" denotes a French-language literature that developed in Canada, especially in the province of Quebec, beginning with travel narratives of the first colonists and extending to works of the present day. The fortunes of this literature have been linked to those of the North American French colony. Consequently, like Canada's French population itself, it has undergone several profound changes of identity throughout time.

Labeled "Canadian" in the eighteenth century (since at the time the term Canadian applied to the French-speaking inhabitants of Canada no matter where they lived, from Lac Saint-Laurent to Windsor), the French-language literature of Canada became "French-Canadian" with the dawn of the Confederation in 1867. From that date on, there have been officially two founding peoples of Canada: the French Canadians and the English Canadians. Beginning in the 1960s with the Quiet Revolution however, this literature acquired a new title: *québécoise.*

The growing autonomy of this literature, although already present in the years shortly following World War II, accelerated with the nationalistic spirit of the 1960s. These years marked the true birth of Quebecois literature, the moment when it separated itself from French literature and when its own criticism developed, with its own loci of reception and approbation.

Prior to this, even though important Canadian works had existed since at least the nineteenth century, French-Canadian literature was simply not taught. To teach French-language literature was rather to teach French literature, "real" literature. Only at the beginning of the twentieth century—and especially during the 1950s—did certain universities introduce courses on French-Canadian literature into French literature departments.[2] At the time it undoubtedly occupied a marginal position in relation to the French corpus, and its instructors were amateurs who, while understanding the political and sociocultural context of the works, lacked fundamental training. With the Quiet Revolution however, Quebecois literature took its revenge on French literature, and from that point on began to occupy a privileged place in literature departments to the degree that, based on the number of

2. Joseph Melançon, *Le discours de l'université sur la littérature québécoise* (Quebec: Nuit blanche, 1996).

courses offered by the programs, it reached equal status with the literature of France.

The factor that determined which French-language works and authors would be taught was strictly territorial—the corpus was limited to texts of Quebecois origin. Such a stipulation clearly excluded French-speaking authors living in different provinces of the country, but the rule was occasionally bypassed in order to incorporate into Quebecois literature the works of various other Canadians writing in French. The growing importance of Quebecois literature, envisioned as a national literature, led to a reconfiguration in the teaching of French literature at the university. What place, however, would other French-language literature occupy next to those of France and Quebec?

Considering the historical situation of instruction in Francophone literatures, a fundamental contradiction becomes apparent in the Quebecois universities. On the one hand, they claim to be the guarantors of the promotion of the French language, while on the other, they consider other French-language literatures as intruders. The push to elevate the teaching of Quebecois literature to the status of a national literature thus implies a withdrawal from the rest of Francophone literature, both Canadian and worldwide.

While political *Francophonie* is seen as an ally in the long and difficult quest of the *Belle Province* for national sovereignty, Francophone literature presents a narrative opposed to the national literary project. It is as if the Quebecois consider themselves—legitimately—as "Francophone" when it comes to politics, but when it comes to teaching French-language literature, they situate themselves deliberately on the margin of the Francophone movement. The Quebecois university can even be seen to exhibit a certain haughtiness similar in all respects to that of its French counterpart: it constitutes itself as the center in relation to which other Francophone literatures must define themselves. The literature is Quebecois and cannot therefore be Francophone.

With specialized centers and numerous research groups in the discipline, Quebecois literature has supplanted French literature at the research level, while the two enjoy a certain parity in the courses offered by Quebecois universities. While undergraduate programs offer an equal number of courses in Quebecois and French literature, the majority of graduate theses and dissertations have subjects taken from Quebecois literature, to the point that it can be considered a marked academic trend. The growing interest in the field is evidently accompanied by a disaffection toward French literature. Although until 1997 the Université Laval was the only university to offer degree programs in Quebecois literature from the bachelor's degree to the doctorate, numerous students at other universities earned independent studies degrees in Quebecois literature.

In fact, the focus on Quebecois literature has continued to grow since the Quiet Revolution. In addition to a nationalistic spirit that very few students resist, this tendency can in part be explained by the influence of the teachers—to be a humanities teacher in the secondary school system of Quebec today is also to teach Quebecois literature, since this literature has gained such importance in the curriculum of French courses, as is evidenced by the time allotted to it. It should also be added that students feel more at home with Quebecois literature than with French literature, even more so because publishing houses, which, especially in Montreal, present a career opportunity for students, require a knowledge of the Quebecois literary establishment.

Certainly the desire to grant Quebecois literature the status that it deserves corresponds to a legitimate ideological need to give it the status of a national literature. However, it creates a danger that is already noticeable to a certain degree in the university setting. Conferring increasing importance to Quebecois literature in the literary training of students introduces a rivalry with French literature and limits the intellectual horizon of the student; privileging only French and Quebecois literature gives the illusion that France and Quebec are the only regions in the world to produce French-language literature.

As can be seen, the Quebecois university has in this matter conducted itself like the French university. It has appropriated other French-language Canadian writers and incorporated them into Quebecois literature just as French literature has tended to do with Belgian and Swiss writers. Sensitivity to other Francophone literatures does not figure into the ideological situation, and the Quebecois university has not opened itself readily to either Francophone literatures or to other fields of knowledge relative to third world countries.

FRANCOPHONE LITERATURES IN QUEBEC, OR THE EXCLUDED THIRD TERM

Looking at the history of Francophone literary instruction in Quebec, two universities have had a noticeable pioneering role in the implementation and development of teaching and research: the Université Laval and the Université de Sherbrooke. By creating the Centre d'Études des

Littératures d'Expression Française (CELEF) and the Éditions Naaman, Professor Antoine Naaman launched the field of Francophone studies at the Université de Sherbrooke. The center enjoyed moments of glory, attracting researchers from America, Europe, and Africa while working to promote and increase awareness of the literatures of the Maghreb, sub-Saharan Africa, the Antilles, and Haiti. Furthering the action of CELEF, the Éditions Naaman constituted another invaluable instrument for the diffusion of *Francophonie*. The publishing house printed documents, dissertations, and creative works from the entire Francophone world. The periodical *Présence francophone* from the same university also played a considerable role in the worldwide dissemination of Francophone literary research.

As for the Université Laval, as the premier French-language university in North America it has always recognized that it has a special mission to preserve and spread French, as well as Francophone, culture. One of its chief priorities has been and continues to be to promote French studies in America. To this fundamental goal the Université Laval has added an additional dimension, that of the study of North American *Francophonie*. While maintaining its large French and Quebecois literature programs, since 1968 the Université Laval has played a key role in the teaching of other Francophone literatures—first the literatures of sub-Saharan Africa and the Maghreb, and subsequently those of Haiti, Switzerland, Belgium, the Antilles, and the Indian Ocean. Instruction in these literatures has been supported at every academic level; more than forty master's theses and twenty doctoral dissertations have been presented and successfully defended.

However, observing the development of instruction in Francophone literatures in Quebec from the 1970s until today, it is evident that progress has been uneven; certain universities have never hired a specialist in the field. From the 1970s to the 1990s the Université Laval and the Université de Sherbrooke gave an important place to instruction and research in the field of Francophone literatures, but by the end of the 1990s the Francophone literatures program was surviving with difficulty at Laval, where only one professor remained of the four who had taught during the preceding decades. At Sherbrooke, the program has been completely abandoned. Not only have the CELEF and the Éditions Naaman been discontinued and the only specialized periodical in the field, *Présence francophone,* been replaced by a review devoted to Quebecois literature, *Les cahiers Anne Hébert,* but no specialist has been hired to succeed Antoine Naaman. In a general sense, this is also the situation in the universities of Quebec outside of Montreal.

On the other hand, in the Montreal universities there is an increasingly pronounced movement toward *Francophonie*. Each one of the city's universities has at least one professor who teaches courses in the field. Furthermore, in certain respects, the Université de Montréal has taken over the leadership role that the Université Laval used to enjoy— the Université de Montréal has hired two specialists to cover the sector, in addition to creating required Francophone undergraduate courses, a seminar each year, and a *Francophonie* specialization in the undergraduate French Studies degree program. During the 1990s, it seems that the other universities of Quebec closed themselves to *Francophonie* at the very moment that those of Montreal, and particularly the Université de Montréal, were embracing it.

TOWARD THE INTEGRATION OF FRANCOPHONE LITERATURES INTO ENGLISH-SPEAKING CANADA

At Canadian English-language universities, the teaching of Francophone literatures has followed a traditional course. In the teaching of French-language humanities, the Canadian university has for a long time granted a large place to French literature, French language, and French culture in a global sense. This vast field traditionally constitutes the domain of French studies.

In teaching and research, the preference has always been to divide the material by centuries to such a degree that one could well deplore the consistent tendency to subordinate textual methods to literary history and, by so doing, to neglect the specifically literary dimension of the texts. French literature is taught in a way that reinforces the ideology of Literature as institution, emphasizing that it functions cohesively with other institutions in the service of the French Nation, producer of a culture and a literature worthy to be taught. The texts are gathered, analyzed, and interpreted in the anthologies and manuals employed in Canadian universities for their so-called literary value, corresponding to the clarity of the "*esprit français.*"

Not until the 1970s did the Canadian universities of the Anglophone provinces begin to give an important place to Quebecois literature and to teach texts from other literatures of the French language: the literatures of Africa, the Antilles, the Maghreb, Belgium, and Switzerland. At first, the somewhat belated discovery of these literatures led to the tendency (still present, to a certain degree) to define "Francophone literatures" as those not French, Quebecois, or French Canadian. From the 1970s to the beginning of the 1980s, the teaching of these literatures had some common characteristics. As a general rule, it was associated with those universities that sought to present themselves as progressive, such as the University of British Columbia at Vancouver, the University of Alberta, the University of Toronto, and York University. On the other hand, these literatures were taught within the framework of introductory courses, which did not allow for extensive study of the literary texts. Occasionally a graduate seminar was offered, but the students only possessed a relatively meager base of information and training in the discipline.

As in Quebec, Francophone literatures in English-speaking Canada occupied a marginal position. Furthermore, in the universities where they were taught, students lacked preparatory instruction about the context or even about the works themselves, as they had never taken a course in the field in secondary school. Despite a sensitivity to fields considered marginal that generally has characterized the Canadian university, Francophone works remained rather poorly represented in the programs of French departments.

However, an abrupt change took place during the 1990s, undoubtedly because of the influence of American universities that spearheaded theoretical movements that tended to promote the teaching of Francophone literatures. Coming from the United States, these theories—postmodernism, deconstruction, women's studies, cultural studies, and postcolonial studies—by the simple fact that they placed in doubt the intellectual logocentrism that had largely characterized the humanities, shook up the cultural homogeneity that prevailed in the various departments of French studies. From this time on, it was the moment of *Francophonie*. Universities competed in the field, and even the departments that could already claim a master's or doctoral program hired one or more additional specialists. In addition to the more progressive universities already mentioned, the French departments in the majority of Canadian Anglophone universities opened up to *Francophonie* by introducing specialized courses and recruiting qualified professors.

Currently, at the undergraduate level, the structure of the curriculum is shaped by the necessity to teach the French language, to give the student a literary training centered in French literature (from the Middle Ages to the twentieth century), and at the same time to provide indispensable exposure to the literatures of *Francophonie*.[3] The program is conceived so that by the end of the fourth year, the student has acquired a knowledge, as broad as possible, of all the general aspects of French literature in addition to taking an average of two to three courses dealing with Francophone and Quebecois literatures.

TO CONCLUDE

Begun in the 1970s, instruction in Francophone literatures has experienced, overall, a continual progression. These literatures are present today in all the major universities of the country, with a few notable exceptions, such as the University of Ottawa, and the entire Université du Québec system (not including the Université du Québec à Montréal). Nevertheless, an analysis of the programs and of faculty specialities clearly shows that *Francophonie* is still a work in progress. It is not perceived as a well-defined field. It also does not enjoy any degree of equality. There persists in Canada and in Quebec, and most likely elsewhere as well, a hierarchical relation between French and Quebecois literature on one side and Francophone literatures on the other. One need only look at the space allotted in the university curriculum for the teaching of these "other literatures" in order to understand the situation. A clear disparity can be observed between the manifest discourse of political *Francophonie* and the daily reality of teaching and research in Francophone literary studies. Moreover, a major difference in the evolution of the phenomenon must be noted: in the whole of the Canadian university network, Francophone literatures are taught more in Anglophone Canada than in Quebec, the country's French-speaking province. It seems that two unrelated developments explain the situation. If at the beginning of the 1990s Francophone literatures in Anglophone Canada experienced exponential growth, it was due to the influence of American universities that were undergoing the same process. At the same time in Quebecois universities, the ideology of nationalism that elevated Quebecois texts to the status of a national literature produced a duality between the French corpus and that of Quebec. Here Francophone literatures appeared as an excluded third term.

    3. Suzanne Crosta, "Considérations con/textuelles et stratégies pédagogiques sur l'enseignement des littératures francophones de l'Afrique et des Antilles," *Tangence* 49 (1995): 78–93.

Examining the analyzed data, it becomes evident that the enthusiasm during the 1970s for these literatures stemmed largely from the euphoria of the newly emerging politics of *Francophonie* in certain areas of Quebec. If the teaching of Francophone literatures was made possible through the generosity and efforts of a certain vanguard, it was never entirely integrated into the priorities of departments. The proof is that, after the retirement of this first generation, no successors followed. On the other hand, the present trend in Francophone literatures, more manifest in Anglophone universities than in their Quebec counterparts, comes from the United States and appears much more integral, due to the politics of the departments involved.

In conclusion, it should be noted that in the universities where they are taught, Francophone literatures no longer need to be justified to students, department administrators, or faculty. Knowledge of these literatures seems to be an increasingly necessary element for a good education in the current framework of globalization, and the immediately accessible context for students and researchers of French studies is the Francophone sphere.

—Translated by Michael Call

FARID LAROUSSI

When Francophone Means National: The Case of the Maghreb

The idea that Francophone studies are made rather than found is beginning to take hold of our imagination in academe. The model has moved from a single type of interpretation (Francophone world as opposed to France) to a multileveled operational system (Francophone distinctions, and differences within national discourses) first and foremost obsessed with finding ways to legitimate its own authority. The case of Francophone literature from the Maghreb demonstrates that the considerable historical, social, or linguistic significance of what France was, and to a certain degree still is, can be displaced. However, the lasting use of French in Algeria, Morocco, and Tunisia should not be underestimated and shows as well that literature from these nations gives an unimpeachable credential to all expressions of power. In a context in which North African peoples are struggling to win a measure of democratic rule and to gain economic independence, the continuous presence of the colonial language has created new cultural forms within each society. This is a paradox that most clearly stands out in the field of literature.

Francophone Maghrebi literature elevates language to the place in culture traditionally held by political discourse, religion, and a sense of identity relevant to both society and the individual. While Arabic (unlike Berber languages) benefits from a high degree of official representation, French allows tactical transgressions in the name of the mother tongue. For instance, the treatment of identity by Algerian or Moroccan Francophone authors is less indicative of a given colonial condition than is that of Francophone Caribbean writers. Yet those Maghrebi novelists strive for self-assertion sometimes at the cost of exile because of their cultural desecration and political subversion. Writing in French can also be an emancipatory experiment putting the individual at the

YFS 103, *French and Francophone*, ed. Farid Laroussi and Christopher L. Miller,
© 2003 by Yale University.

center of the discourse in a way that shuns the epistemology of the group so emblematic of Islamic culture.

On the other hand, a text in the Arabic tradition was supposed to embody the spirit of Islam, literally to form one body with the community or *ummah.* The writer was the representative and a harbinger of the canon. Texts became extensions of interpretative agreements within the world of arts and the society at large. In the 1930s a new movement emerged in the Near East, in Egypt in particular, firmly putting forward a need for change in all aspects of Arab culture. The *nahda,* or renaissance, as it was called, set no definite bounds. Yet it moved away from a traditional culture that had long lost its transformative powers, as well as away from colonial influences. Language and literary paradigms were indeed modernized but the models were set in and by Middle-Eastern cultures, mainly Egyptian and Lebanese. In the case of the Maghreb, literary texts in Arabic rarely reflected the actual societies. First, written Arabic was only remotely connected with the form of the language spoken throughout North Africa. Second, the novel, although a genre inherited from the European tradition, originated in the Middle East, turning it into the source of high culture. Finally, books, particularly novels, were and still are for a large part published in Cairo or Beirut, although there are burgeoning publishing houses in the largest cities throughout the Maghreb. It becomes apparent that in the three countries of the Maghreb neither French nor classical Arabic is congruent with culture.[1]

These are contradictory shiftings and conflicting relationships that appear in literary productions, not as a matter of degree but of substance. When Rachid Boudjedra, for example, tried his hand at writing novels in Arabic, his talent at dismantling values and denouncing the madness of a society still in search of itself got entangled in pre-existing cultural categorizations (official history, the crisis of sexuality, religious injunctions, sociolinguistic limitations) that stifled his literary imagination. After a few attempts he eventually reverted to French. Francophone writers have often been blamed for writing for a Maghrebi elite strictly educated in French, if not for European readers. Authors who write in Arabic, for their part, are confronted with the dilemma of being acknowledged by other Arab cultures while their works bear little relation to their putative objects, that is, Algerian, Moroccan, or

---

1. It must be noted, however, that the use of Arabic or French varies greatly according to social classes, gender groups, and regions of residence.

Tunisian cultures. The writers' condition is all the more dramatic since Maghreb nations still seem in search of their cultural independence, which is neither French nor Arabic, in spite of the official mantras of Pan-Arabism from the Middle-East, or *Francophonie* inclusion from France and its institutions. Two different literatures coexist and hedge their bets as to how to define their identities and roles, while at the same time they advertise their special ties to Europe and the Middle-East.

In the specific case of Francophone authors, the constitution of knowledge and the systems of reference are essentially different from those that were inherited from Eurocentric discourse. For instance, one could read Mohammed Dib's *Le métier à tisser* (1957) as a reply to Camus's *La peste* (1947). To speak then, simplistically, of choosing one language over another is to elide the issue of double perspective. On the one hand, the Francophone point of view holds that an author creates with language, and on the other, Maghrebi cultural crises are what an author is prepared to write about.[2] Yet such a process enables imagination even as it produces alienation. The negation in this dialectic lies in the fact that Francophone writers are perceived in their homelands as those who broke away from the ideals of independence (myths of origin, national culture, historical legitimacy, and so on) and from the tenets of Arab-Islamic culture, which are brought to the forefront in times of national crises. The case of Algeria in the 1990s illustrates the situation of Francophone authors who were left with no choice but to flee or remain outside the country due to the death sentences passed on them by fundamentalist groups.[3] One of the ironies is that the strongest religious party chose a French acronym, the FIS (*Front Islamique du Salut*), to underscore the very idea that it stands against everything French. Indeed, choosing Arabic would have probably excluded it from mainstream politics. French was and still is a "natural" language in Algeria,[4] yet the country has consistently rejected calls to join the organization of Francophone nations.

2. This is particularly true of first generation Francophone writers. In the 1950s and 1960s the preoccupations for Driss Chraïbi, Mohamed Dib, or Kateb Yacine, for example, were mostly about a semiotics of independence centered on the father figure (real father, ancestor, God-figure, political power, French hegemony, and so on).
3. Rachid Boudjedra, Assia Djebar, Mouloud Mammeri, and Rachid Mimouni, for instance.
4. The first national speech of Abdelaziz Bouteflika, after he was appointed President in April of 1999, was in French.

While the colonial process in the Maghreb generated an imperialist literature as early as the mid 1800s in Algeria,[5] much of the postindependence literary production by Francophone authors cannot be called alienated or nomadic simply because it is generally produced in the former colonial power. The very idea of *another side* of the Mediterranean as the legitimate locus for literary culture raises explicit doubts about the assumptions underlying the traditional junction between narrative, language, and territory.[6] The competing issues do not take place between either a center (Maghreb) or the margins (France/Europe), but rather within the subject him-/herself. Regardless of the focus of the discourses, on ethnicity (Arab/Berber), on religion (Islam/atheism), on gender, on ideologies, or on social classes, Francophone writers are not in a "minor"[7] position. On the contrary, Maghrebi literary works seek to demonstrate that it is not possible to essentialize one particular site of expression, or one value-laden struggle. More often than not, cultural labels (Francophone, exiled, nomad, minority writer) help evade demands for identity. Maghrebi Francophone literature debunks the idea of correspondences by subverting definitional terms such as ideology, humanism, market, religion, identity, power, democracy, subjectivity, and so forth. When Assia Djebar addresses the issues of women and Islam in her fiction, she does hold current Algerian values to account. Not only do her women protagonists transform the neocolonial status quo, but they make gender relationships more vulnerable by questioning Algerian national independence and its myth of the revolution, as well as that of the individual as male hero, martyr, or woman rendered

5. A great majority of these early works were military accounts or essays from the social sciences perspective. The first pieces of fiction written by European authors born in Algeria appeared at the end of the nineteenth century and on into the next (Eckmann-Chatrian, Pierre Coeur, Marcel Frescali, Vigné d'Octon, Robert Randau, Magali Boisnard, Elissa Rhaïs, Louis Lecoq). For most of them the purpose of their writings was to glorify the French mission in North Africa, as well as to occupy a field mostly taken up by writers from the *métropole* who visited Algeria and wrote more outstanding works (Flaubert, Maupassant, Gautier, Daudet, Jammes, Gide, Montherlant).

6. In his *Location of Culture* (London: Routledge, 1994), Homi K. Bhabha argues that even during colonial times language and identification were subject to negotiation and resistance from the colonized.

7. The formulation comes from Gilles Deleuze and Félix Guattari's *Mille plateaux* (Paris: Minuit, 1975) in reference to Kafka's work. It does not apply to most Francophone writers because they deny the concept of heterogeneity advocated by Deleuze and Guattari. Francophone literature from the Maghreb is mostly based on stability and constant self-identification.

invisible. At the same time, Assia Djebar's books dispense with the picture of a language intervening between Algerian reality and the exiled self.[8] This is precisely because of the impermanence of the cultural imaginary in a country courted by international paradigms without participation or means.[9] In his novels, Abdlehak Serhane denounces an oppressive economic system that maintains more than half of the Moroccan population in unbearable living conditions, and he depicts the consequences in the construction of emotional and political identities. This sense of political mission impels authors to answer in the negative the question: Could you write in any other language than French? But as they do so, one may wonder if they are not undermining their own project because they fail to engage in two cultural spheres. For readers in the Maghreb, Francophone literature unfolds more like a metaphor of substitution than one of addition. In spite of the decades of independence, there are still people who speak French who live in conditions better than those of readers in the Maghreb and who lecture them about what is good for them. The cruel irony is that Maghrebi Francophone writing is a wandering language that becomes lost the closer it gets to home.

Yet the issue of language remains altogether crucial, for resistance to France is still the working of a colonial ideology, only this time from the former colonized. Francophone literature is conceived from a position of power that lacks a point of origin. It is from this position that the democratic dimension embraces the act of writing because it belongs to everyone.[10] Whereas different regimes in the Maghreb, with the exception of Tunisia, have overplayed the Arabic language card at critical stages (the 1970s in Morocco, the 1990s in Algeria), Francophone literature has become the ultimate tool for questioning the Enlightenment, notably its ideology that helped perpetuate humanistic

8. Her crypto-autobiographical novel *Ombre sultane* proceeds from the urgency to recast the fundamental role of women in modern Algeria, while Djebar's specular style zeros in on her own absence. See Assia Djebar, *Ombre sultane* (Paris: Albin Michel, 1987).

9. The influence of television, with the proliferation of satellite dishes and of the migrant population (mainly in France), contributes to such a schizoid conception of sociocultural realities, in Algeria as well as in its two Maghrebi neighbors.

10. In this case the concept of origin refers to the fact that hardly any Maghrebi writer places him-/herself in a particular French literary tradition. Through such a resistance these writers become their own origins, and so literature itself has no origin but spills over beyond any specific delineations and Western taxonomies.

self-images, and its muted repressive colonial structures.[11] The fact
that only in June of 1999 did France recognize that what happened in
Algeria from 1954 until 1962 was a "war" highlights the contradictions
at the core of its so-called enlightened values.[12] Francophone literature
is also poststructural inasmuch as it strives to foreground its singularity within the scope of the French language, underscoring the fact that
formal/objective paradigms have been dissolved in the questioning of
Western as well as Arab-Islamic values. For example, it is most obvious all through Kateb's work in his discourse on "les Ancêtres" and the
history of Eastern Algeria. In the same way, Djebar exposes the ideology of colonialism in *L'amour, la fantasia,* or provides an unequivocal
account of the Islamic tradition from the point of view of women in
Loin de Médine.

Although Francophone writers from the Maghreb are somewhat indebted to traveling theories such as Marxism, structuralism, or postcolonialism,[13] the fact remains that their use of the French language
does not so much override its humanistic content as it negates the historicity and ends of the colonial language itself. Little wonder that on
a purely conceptual basis their works do not invoke, let alone exalt,
French literature *per se.*

As a matter of fact, the French language helps empower ties with
the Maghrebi mother culture because more often than not, for younger
generations of writers, it does not come as a choice but stems from a
specific context (the social background, the region of origin, the position of French in the respective education systems). To some extent,
Francophone literature fulfills its conflicting purposes by reformulating

11. The best examples in this regard are Camus's novels, which rest upon a cancel-
ing out or dissolution of Algerian identity. It is ironic that in the 1990s Camus became
for some Algerian writers (Boudjedra, Djebar, or Sebbar) a moral figure set up against all
forms of fundamentalism, while his own record on the Algerian War was quite disap-
pointing at best.
12. It is interesting to note that after this official recognition the nation was shaken
by debates about the widespread use of torture during the Algerian War and the question
of assigning responsibility. Eventually Prime Minister Lionel Jospin decided that it was
a matter that needed to be settled by historians rather than political institutions, which
was an indirect way of answering the question about responsibility.
13. Edward Said was one of the first scholars to propose and develop the concept of
traveling theories, especially in his book *The World, the Text, and the Critic* (Cambridge,
MA: Harvard University Press, 1983), chapter 10, "Traveling Theory." He opposes the local and the singular to the global and the totality, so that the intellectual (scholar, novelist, and so on) can occupy a critical position within the paradigms of the dominant culture, whether it is Western or a power system in a third-world country.

the crisis of the author's subjectivity. In fact, it is not unusual that those Francophone Maghrebi intellectuals with third-world sensibilities and first-world orientations provide a point of critical distance that cannot appear in a strictly Western perspective,[14] which is often keen to maintain a totalizing approach to literature and culture. For instance, instead of working within exclusively "Western" literary movements or ideological discourses, Francophone writers try to resolve the problems of constructing their literature within a context of relativism. Kateb gives an Algerian reply to a Marxist question about history and independence. Djebar incorporates French feminism into a genealogical mode of inquiry of Islam. Khatibi is interested in the operations of language as it is emptied of its cultural capital, especially the assimilation of the Maghreb as an extension of French culture.

The upshot of this way of mapping an absent cultural space through intellectual intentions, while a very large majority of Francophone writers live in exile, is to effect significant exclusions. One example of this is the silencing of their Arab (and Berber) counterparts who also write fiction but are caught between the effects of the French colonial *tabula rasa* on Arab deculturation on the one hand, and a hegemonic Middle East that prescribes the centrality of Arabic on the other. It is no wonder that Francophone writers, although they pay a substantial price, have become the "establishment" of Maghrebi literature. In sum, while Francophone authors resist forms of subjection both in their homelands and inside French culture, they still need to disassociate themselves from political praxis and economic demands[15] in order to remake themselves not as *Francophone* but as Algerian, Moroccan, or Tunisian writers.

This last point highlights the more technical aspects of the issue. Stretching the French language beyond its normal bounds is insufficient: it needs to be deconstructed out of its own preconditions, one of which is irremediably associated with the publishing process. As Paris

14. It seems that there are writers who simply live in exile (mostly in France), and those who have reached privileged positions within Western academe (France and North America).

15. Too often Arab culture and Islam in particular are harnessed inside a pro-West discourse. Whether it is intended or not, this seems like a pathology of reversed colonialism in which French linguistic achievements unashamedly downplay those of the Maghrebi mother culture. As for economic considerations, they are informed by publishing houses or sometimes political contexts, as when Tahar Ben Jelloun, in 2000, was paid more than half a million French francs to begin writing a book about the story of a former Moroccan political prisoner.

is the capital of the exiled community of Maghrebi writers, the most significant and troubling thing about that condition is that by settling into the former *métropole,* authors have become involved in an abnormal enterprise. Francophone authors succumb to what I dub deterritorialization through imperialism. Language is itself the point of contact, but the discursive practices bear all the marks of editorial supervision from Paris. For instance, it is quite puzzling that all through the 1990s Algerian women writing about the condition of Algerian women in their homeland were welcomed by French publishing houses.[16] The origin of the discourse was no longer the Maghreb but France, where exoticism has been reinvented and the orientalist paradigm survives. The sociopolitical situation in Algeria rightly comes under attack but only as a way to reassert France's own representation as a land of Enlightenment. In this sense, Francophone literature can be both liberating and smothering, depending on which postnational condition is invoked or denied. It is no wonder that in the 1990s, while Algerian literature was all the rage, Francophone writings by Moroccan and Tunisian authors found it difficult to attract any attention at all in France.

To grasp the scope of Francophone literature and its assumed national content, it is important to see beyond isolated artistic practices. The fact of the matter is that in Algeria, Morocco, and Tunisia the French language is viewed according to different sets of political and cultural agendas. While Tunisia tentatively solved the issue by embracing a bilingual system (Arabic/French) as early as the 1960s, the two other nations have been struggling ever since independence, with far less satisfactory results. Both in Algeria and Morocco academic programs of Arabization have been failures, for three main reasons. One is that by the late twentieth century, Arabic had ceased to be a world language because its political potency and economic prominence had seriously diminished. Second, school programs were generally taught by visiting professors from the Middle East, whose task was to force-feed Maghrebi students a language that was familiar yet culturally foreign.

16. Authors such as Feriel Assima, Latifah Ben Mansour, Maissa Bey, Malika Boussouf, Nina Hayat, Naila Imaksen, Leila Marouane, Malika Mokeddem, or Hafsa Zinaï-Koudil have in common the fact that they are all women, they were published in France in the 1990s, and they are writing about women in Algeria. While the literary value of their respective works can be discussed at length, such a conjunction of facts and themes questions the value of Maghrebi Francophone literature as a postcolonial commodity produced in France for French readers.

Last, the politics of Arabization have been erratic, too often associated with short-term political gains, either by showing the nation's cultural independence from France, or by trying to woo voters from the religious wing. Sometimes the situation verges on public schizophrenia, like in Morocco where Arabic has been the only official administrative language since 1990, while in business and in the mainstream media French is the only *lingua franca*. Although the Moroccan public system of education is officially bilingual (Arabic/French), the future elite is still educated in private schools which are in large majority French run, although American institutions are beginning to spread and exercise considerable influence. Since 1992 the Algerian people have been paying the price of a horrendous civil war waged between gangs of religious fundamentalists and the military establishment that has unofficially clung to power since Boumediène's coup in 1965.

These ten years of struggle have shaped the conflict about the presence and the function of French versus Arabic. As a result, many university departments of French studies have closed or have drastically reduced their teaching loads. In Algiers, a *fatwa*[17] was declared against faculty who taught French. As a consequence the university department lost 60 percent of its members to early retirement or forced exile to Europe or Canada.[18] In high schools French was downgraded to "a foreign language," on a par with English or Spanish, although everything from applied sciences, to history, to literature used to be taught in French. Furthermore, the French Cultural Centers, essential providers of information on current cultural events (press, films, books, exhibitions) for the residents of the largest cities, have all closed since 1993. One reopened in Annaba in 2000 under heavy protection. At the same time, twelve of the sixteen dailies and weeklies that are published in Algiers are in French. Overall, when one considers the history of Algeria since independence (forty years ago), the schooling programs, however disjointed they have been, have done more for the promotion of the French language than France ever did during its one hundred and thirty-two years of occupation. This is a troubling fact that hampers any quest for national wholeness and identity.

17. A *fatwa* is a nonbinding legal opinion, traditionally regarding questions of jurisprudence, or religious interpretations. After the Islamic Revolution in Iran in 1979, *fatwas* have been given a decisively more militant meaning.
18. In May and June of 2001, I had the opportunity, generously provided by a Yale-Griswold Fellowship, to visit Algeria (and Morocco) and personally witness the deplorable state of French studies in three universities.

In such contexts the status of the French language in general, and Francophone literature in particular, can be viewed as uncertain. Especially in Algeria, more and more Francophone works are studied from a sociohistorical perspective, mostly as third-world literature, rarely as national literature. It is easy to point out that from the Southern shore of the Mediterranean, *francophonie* is defined along political terms rather than cultural or theoretical ones. The loss of faith in independence affects the national cultural projects that should include Francophone literature. The revival of ethnic claims (Arabs versus Berbers) and of religious fundamentalism can be interpreted as a response to radical doubt focused on the questions of unity and identity. Bypassing oral traditions, Francophone literature has become a transnational affair as well as the expression of a discourse on fragmentation (subject versus community). Another element that renders Francophone writers marginal *at home* is that publishing policies are decided in France. Therefore the authors find themselves uprooted from their native land, twice over: first as exiles, and second as nonparticipants in the national cultural configuration. It is true as well that the issue of readership is overwhelming. All throughout the Maghreb most people do not read books, because they are too expensive, because of still high illiteracy rates,[19] or simply because widespread violence[20] puts too high a premium on literature as a cultural artefact. Education and social stability may not be enough, but they do help empower people. Nonetheless, amid unmanageable challenges a question lingers: how can such a disjunctive place as the Maghreb produce such fruitful crops of writers?

19. According to World Bank statistics, in 1999 the illiteracy rates for adults were a little more than 65 percent in Algeria, nearly 80 percent in Morocco, and about 60 percent in Tunisia. The hidden truth behind these figures is that illiteracy affects first and foremost women, and that it besets speakers of both languages, Arabic and French.

20. Under the rule of Ben Ali, the self-proclaimed President, Tunisia has become a police state, in Morocco chronic poverty is the worst kind of violence (it has the lowest GDP of all three countries), and in Algeria institutional repression and pervasive corruption are tantamount to governmental insanity.

III. Impact, Influence, and Interpretation

J. MICHAEL DASH

Caraïbe Fantôme: The Play of Difference in the Francophone Caribbean*

What we normally call "local color" is simply that specificity, that
difference in its most striking manifestation.
        —Michel Leiris, "Antilles and Poetry at the Crossroads"

Our imagination had been inhabited by all the forms of vegetation
that le Douanier Rousseau had predicted.
        —Édouard Glissant, *Faulkner, Mississippi*

In their unprecedented examination of the passage of the French Surrealists through the Caribbean during the 1940s, *Refusal of the Shadow*,
Michael Richardson and Kyzystof Fijalkowski point out that these
"unique encounters" between Surrealists fleeing a war-torn Europe during World War II and Francophone Caribbean writers "have been little
studied in the English-speaking world." Their contention is that these
encounters raise "subtle and important questions with multifarious implications for current debates concerning alterity and communication
between cultures."[1] They may have underestimated the importance of
what they had observed, since one would be hard put to find, even in
French, a thoroughgoing examination of this period of interaction between a French avant-garde and Caribbean writers. Indeed, it is arguable
in this period of global dislocation and unprecedented hemispheric contact that Caribbean literature faced the full implications of its mod-

---

*This is a revised and expanded version of "The Madman at the Crossroads: Delirium
and Dislocation in Caribbean Literature," *Profession 2002* (New York: Modern Language
Association): 37–43.
    1. Michael Richardson and Krzyztof Fijalkowski, *Refusal of the Shadow* (London:
Verso, 1996), 1.

YFS 103, *French and Francophone,* ed. Farid Laroussi and Christopher L. Miller,
© 2003 by Yale University.

ernist legacy and established itself self-consciously within inter-American space. The question of the irreducible alterity of other cultures and the radical interrogation of narrative discursive positions, raised in the context of these encounters, arguably created a new hemispheric subjectivity in the imaginary of the writers of the region.

This new transnational perspective complicated their relation with the totalizing categories of French or what would later be known as "Francophone."[2] The framing of ideas of cultural difference, specificity, and reciprocity in the 1940s had much to do with the Surrealists' experience of exile in the Americas. Their traveling at the time connected the French Caribbean, Haiti, and Cuba with South America and may well have placed New York at the center of a new cultural triangle in the New World, almost completely effacing colonial and anticolonial paradigms. It firmly established as a new literary project, what could previously have been seen as merely an adjunct to writing in French, and this project could henceforth only be fully understood within a cross-cultural hemispheric perspective.

The tendency has been so far to link the influence of Surrealism almost exclusively to Aimé Césaire and his brand of Negritude, particularly because of the primitivist poetics and the techniques of radical juxtaposition used in Césaire's poetry. No attention is paid to the travel writing of the Surrealists, which influenced the post-Negritude generation of writers. The passage of the Surrealists, in particular André Breton and Pierre Mabille, through the Caribbean in the 1940s inaugurated a form of travel writing that broke with the refusal of specificity and descriptive prose championed in Breton's 1925 manifesto. This writing arguably launched a new anthropological discourse that would mark the major innovative tendencies in Caribbean writing in French from the 1950s onwards. In their journeys, fleeing Vichy-dominated France, Breton and Mabille did not encounter an uncontaminated elsewhere in the Caribbean. Rather, they came upon lands marked by Europe's past colonial adventures where present political crises were reproduced in a tropical locale. Also, estranged as they were from their own cultural origins, these chastened revolutionaries were more open to questioning their own utopian cultural reflexes, accepting the interplay of cultural difference and discovering themselves through the other societies they encountered.

2. As late as 1954, Auguste Viatte could classify writing in French from the Caribbean as "littérature de l'Amérique française," which, with its "émotivité nègre," was a mere adjunct to literature from the *métropole*. See Viatte, *Histoire littéraire de l'Amérique française des origines à 1950* (Paris: PUF, 1954).

The key to understanding the exemplary sensitivity of the travel narratives of the Surrealists in the Caribbean in the 1940s lies perhaps in the earlier journey of Michel Leiris through Africa. In 1931 Leiris took part in an ethnographic expedition through Africa, an account of which he kept in a voluminous diary entitled "De Dakar à Djibouti (1931–1933)." This work was eventually published under the title *Afrique fantôme*, not simply because it was a more attractive choice for a title, but because of the author's dismaying realization that the Africa he set out to find was never there. In an indirect way, this work is tied to the Caribbean, since Leiris was first fascinated by William Seabrook's luridly sensationalist account of Haitian vodun, *The Magic Island*.[3] He finds in his journey from the Atlantic to the Red Sea that he cannot reproduce the primitivist narrative of a Seabrook. He then questions the possibility of this kind of ethnographic knowledge of the other and his narrative turns into field notes about himself. James Clifford points to this element that marks Leiris's text when he observes

> *L'Afrique fantôme* begins a writing process that will endlessly pose and recompose an identity. Its poetics is one of incompletion and process, with space for the extraneous. Interrupting the smooth ethnographic story of an access to Africa, it undermines the assumption that self and other can be gathered in a stable narrative coherence.[4]

The antinarrative of *Afrique fantôme* could be seen as poor amateurish ethnography, but it is an exemplary model for Surrealist travel writing. The discontinuous nature of the narrative, the openness to objective chance, and most of all the displacement of the object of ethnographic study acquire a new urgency for Breton and Mabille in their accounts of their journeys through the Caribbean in the 1940s. Africa remains elusive but real for Leiris, irreducibly other, an absence that resists being grounded in an ethnographic discourse. The journal turns inward and focuses on the traveler's own imaginative processes, becoming a self-ethnography that tracks the writers self-doubts and anxieties and a "succession of flashes related to objective facts as much as

3. Leiris's contacts with the Caribbean grew in the 1940s when he visited Haiti on an invitation from the French Institute in Port-au-Prince. He also published, in 1955, a report on Martinique and Guadeloupe for UNESCO entitled *Contacts de civilization en Martinique et en Guadeloupe*, which, because of its detailed observations, has won high praise from Édouard Glissant in *Traité du Tout-Monde* (Paris: Gallimard, 1997), 131.

4. James Clifford, *The Predicament of Culture* (Cambridge: Harvard University Press, 1988), 173.

to external things (lived, seen or heard about)."[5] This account of a journey of futility and self-interrogation through a zone of elusive specificity can be seen as an important precursor to Breton's *Martinique charmeuse de serpents*, which probably could have been called "Martinique fantôme."

Breton's account of his arrival in Martinique in 1941 en route to exile in North America is every bit as strange a travel narrative as Leiris's earlier crossing of the African continent. Part reportage, part poetry, part encomium to Césaire, Breton's book, as Leiris himself in his review of this work observes, acquires a truth—in its use of poetry, drawing, and disconnected fragments—superior to that of "the descriptive style typical of the majority of specialists of the travel narrative . . . which appears quite flawed because of its characteristic external perspective (without going so far as to mention their temptation to fiddle with reality)."[6] Like Leiris, Breton sets out to find a mythical, exotic Martinique: "[W]ith what avidity did I plunge into the streets, in search of all the never-before-seen things they had to offer, the dazzle of the markets, the humming-bird accents, the women Paul Eluard, on his return from a trip around the world, had told me were more beautiful than anywhere else." He finds, however, to his dismay, that this is an island of shipwrecks, both literal and metaphorical. His view is initially blocked by "the hulk of a ship" from which he wrests himself free only to be confronted by the wreck of the town: "all movement was a little slower than might have been necessary, all sound too distinct, as if something had run aground." Césaire's poem offers a moment of illumination in this world of shadows, but the presence of the concentration camp, the Vichy government, and the wreckage of the colonial past make it impossible for Breton to lay claim discursively to this tropical space.

The foregrounding of self-doubt, the inability to produce a stable travel narrative, and the inward-turning tendency of the text are dramatically illustrated in the section "Dialogue créole" in which the slipperiness of representation is reflected on in a text that is at once a dialogue between Masson and Breton, the traveler and the landscape, and the real in the face of the imagined. The complexities and contradictions of representation are pondered in the painting of Le Douanier Rousseau that gives the book its title. Neither Breton nor Masson (one

---

5. Michel Leiris, *Miroir de l'Afrique* (Paris: Gallimard, 1996), 89. Here and throughout, translations are my own unless indicated otherwise.
6. Leiris, *Zébrage* (Paris: Gallimard, 1992), 90.

is never sure who is speaking) mentions that it is not certain that
Rousseau ever saw Martinique or the tropics. However, the painting
contains a mystery that the tropical landscape cannot exhaust. The se-
crets of the Martinique landscape are hidden in this painting and cannot be revealed by a naturalistic account. The Surrealists are nevertheless tempted to fix the baroque luxuriance of the world around them
as if they were latter-day disciples of Rousseau. The Martinican heart-
land is evoked in a theatrically exuberant fantasy. "Yes, our heart is at
the center of this prodigious entanglement. What ladders for dreams
these implacable lianas are and these branches, what bows drawn for
the arrows of our thoughts!"[7]

Just when they are tempted to yield to this lyrical exploitation of
untamed nature, they recall that at the other end of the island there is
another island, a monolith called Diamond Rock that, in its luminous
yet obscure nature, defies discursive control. "Don't you find it at the
same time extraordinary and necessary that the rock of the island that
leads to the open sea should be called precisely Diamond Rock?"[8] They
do not pursue this image much further in 1941. Later Breton would return to it in the monolithic Percé rock in *Arcane 17*. However, in their
brief reference to Diamond Rock, Breton and Masson seem alert to the
way in which the irreducibly opaque object of Diamond Rock liberates
the island space of Martinique from fixed, originary meanings. As with
his attempt to look beyond the shipwreck to find exotic Martinique, he
is again frustrated. The luminous opacity of Diamond Rock and the liberating frame of the sea, with its potential openness to multiple meanings, free the island from a predetermined colonialist discourse. This
insistence on decentering the subject and the refusal to silence the referent are examples of the specialized use by the Surrealists of "le hasard
objectif" (objective chance) within a colonial context. In accepting the
otherness of things, in construing things as freed subjects, the Surrealists are preparing the ground for accepting otherness as such. The dialogic impulse in "Dialogue créole" is ultimately about endowing space
with a new autonomy, conferring a welcome strangeness on all things
and opening new ways of connecting newly liberated opacities. The fa-
cilitating shipwreck, the rock of contradictions, historical fossil and at
the same time totem of a new encounter between secular and sacred,
Diamond Rock/Wreck is emblematic of what Leiris understands as the

7. André Breton, *Martinique charmeuse de serpents*, (Paris: Pauvert, 1972), 93, translation taken from *Refusal of the Shadow* op. cit., 191.
   8. Ibid., 29. *Refusal of the Shadow*, 189.

salutary concreteness in local color and what Édouard Glissant would later call the other's "right to opacity."

The similarities between "Dialogue créole" and Pierre Mabille's "Memories of Haiti" are also quite striking. Like Breton in *Martinique charmeuse de serpents*, Mabille, who had sought refuge in Haiti in the 1940s, is also a Surrealist-ethnographer whose shifting narrative refuses to fix the other. Again, as was the case with Breton whose contact with the *Tropiques* group made Martinique more than just an exotic landscape, Mabille's stay in Haiti coincided with efforts of Haitian intellectuals, led by Jacques Roumain, to save Haitian cultural artifacts from the depredations of the Catholic Church, which was vigorously pursuing its campaign against vodun at the time.[9] The threat of the destruction of Haiti's pre-Columbian past as well as its rich folk culture by self-righteous representatives of the French priests of the Roman Catholic Church provoked the need to institutionalize ethnology as a basis for Haitian national identity. It is in this atmosphere of the pillage of Haitian folk culture in the name of civilization and the attendant need to salvage a national identity that Mabille raises the complex matter of constructing a Haitian cultural specificity.

Mabille's travel narratives are neither a nativist glorification of Haitian folk culture, as was the tendency of some associated with the "Bureau d'ethnologie" at the time, nor are they manifestations of primitivist nostalgia for Haiti's timeless past. They are really field notes of an impossible quest, as the Haiti he sees is a dynamic society haunted by old and new, mysterious and modern. In "Memories of Haiti" he responds to an invitation to witness a vodun ceremony outside of the capital in Leogane, with a group from the recently formed "Bureau d'ethnologie." The naïve interplay of familiar and strange in Mabille's account yields no coherent knowledge and ultimately problematizes the whole project of the anthropological expedition. His tale is framed by the image of the forest as elusive space about which he makes the following perceptive remarks. "Don't we speak of 'plunging into the forest,' don't we talk about its depths, as we would about the depths of a mine or an ocean, and yet it has neither a surface nor a skin, but an edge, a border. Language, confusing the part with the whole, often

9. In his foreword to *Voodoo in Haiti* (London: Andre Deutsch, 1959), Alfred Metraux explains that the idea of the "Bureau of Ethnology" was born out of discussions with Roumain after witnessing the destructive effects of the Catholic Church's campaign against popular religion.

evokes the heart of the forest, doubtless suggesting the meaning of 'heart of the tree,' of a center. But the point is that the forest does not have a center, it is everywhere and nowhere."[10] The forest, as an ambiguous zone of encounter that is less about center and depth than about thresholds and borders, is continuously invoked in an adventure that eventually yields no vodun ceremony but a series of puzzling incidents that provide no way of defining Haitian folk religion.

We do not know whether the consistent mechanical failure of their vehicle is related to the wrath of the loas (supernatural beings in the vodun religion), whether the possession of a secretary at the "Bureau d'ethnologie" is credible or how the immaculately dressed, apparently "alienated" Haitian ethnographer who accompanies them maintains his complete equilibrium in the rain and mud. Their native informant and guide, Dieu-Loué, gets hopelessly lost, and the detailed images Mabille includes of the bustling roadways of rural Haiti reveal a pragmatic culture more involved in its daily survival than in putting on spectacles for eager visitors. In Mabille's account we see the same "poetics of incompletion" that has marked these unstable narratives. The text has that now familiar openness to arbitrary events, inscrutable reality, attention to concrete detail and self-ethnography in which subjectivity is precariously located between a tentative narrative certitude and the invasive play of difference.

What we have been looking at so far is the importance of the ideal of alterity or objectification to the deconstructive travel narratives of the Surrealists in the 1940s. This is not otherness translated or repacked for home consumption but a rehabilitative reification that introduces a new way of conceiving otherness in terms of self-invention, without being seduced or repulsed by it. The importance of this perspective will not be lost on a generation of Caribbean writers from Martinique, Guadeloupe, and Haiti who use the ideal of irreducible opacity as a way of upsetting the symmetries of global encounter and breaking the binaries that we assemble at its crossroads. "The right to opacity" then becomes a mode of resistance that disrupts bland synthesis, that resists being absorbed into hegemonic discourses whether colonial, anticolonial, or postcolonial. While for Césaire and his generation, Surrealism, in a heroic earlier phase, meant the revelation of a universal ideal of the human psyche in which all thought is "one and indivisible," for a later generation Surrealism would usher in the con-

10. Pierre Mabille, *Message de l'étranger* (Paris: Plasma, 1981), 8.

cept of radical plurality and the possibility of using unprecedented ways (traces, detours) of connecting or negotiating the irreducible strangeness of things.

It is within such a context that the work of the largely ignored Haitian writer Magloire St. Aude becomes significant. Clément Magloire (the poet's real name) was singled out, like Césaire, for special praise by Breton but was very much an ideological loner in the 1940s. He neither followed the historical and materialist analysis of Haitian culture of such Marxists as Roumain, nor did he espouse the politics of racial authenticity advocated by his contemporary François Duvalier. He remained at the edge of the ethnological movement and was the target of direct criticism from Roumain, who described his enigmatic verse as "negative and anarchist."[11] St. Aude's dense, elliptical poetry reveals a very different use of Surrealist poetics from that of Aimé Césaire. His is not the dream of homecoming, of sensual contact with the material world. Rather, his work obsessively charts the precarious space of the subject and the invasive force of external reality. His 1941 collection of poems *Dialogue de mes lampes* (Dialogue of my lamps) clearly demonstrates the extent to which the heroic modernist subject of Césairean verse, for instance, has been replaced by a persona, who, incapable of naming and fixing reality, glides through a world of primordial obscurity.

> Je glisse, je descends, je m'enlise
> Dans la laine de mon coma
> Bon comme le lait de la sieste
> Rien n'est moi
> Hormis mes orbites en ogive[12]
>
> (I slide, I go down, I sink
> into the wool of my coma
> good like the milk of a siesta
> I am nothing
> Outside of my arched sockets)

Later works such as *Ombres et reflets* (Shadows and Reflections) (1952) are fragmentary prose texts that seem to fall between intimate journal and documentary narrative. They can be seen as psychic travel narratives, which demonstrate the observer's or, often, the flaneur's

---

11. See Roumain's preface to Edris St. Amand's *Essai d'explication de* Dialogues de mes lampes (Port-au-Prince: Imprimerie de l'État, 1942).

12. Magloire St. Aude, *Dialogue de mes lampes* (Paris: Première Personne, 1970), 22.

anxiety before the object. Slack, drifting, the narrative is open to arbitrary banalities and the desultory recording of people, objects, and fantasies. The very last work St. Aude published, the short story "Veillée" (Vigil) in 1956, dramatizes the narrator's paralysis before the corpse of a young woman. It is ostensibly about zombification but seems also to point to a major preoccupation of St. Aude's, the swarming of the material world, which resists conscious control, the radiant corpse before the dehumanized observer.

> But as I examined her face . . . something caused me to shiver: the eyes were not completely closed and, from beneath the eyelids the dead girl seemed to be looking at me . . . and to look at me with such fixity that filled me with a sense of panic. I tried to move but an intolerable cramp paralyzed my movements. I wanted to speak but was voiceless.
> In the half-light that followed, Teresa opened her eyes wide.[13]

The materializing of the world's elemental strangeness can also be traced in the early writing of Édouard Glissant, whose frequently overlooked book of essays *Soleil de la conscience* seems to consciously adopt the form of the loose travel narratives of the Surrealists. Part poetry, part prose, *Soleil de la conscience,* written in 1955, functions as a travel journal as much as a meditation on the nature of poetry. Glissant's journey is neither one of exile in the *métropole* nor one of return to his island home. It is a work that ultimately deals with the ambiguities and tensions of individual identity. The text permits a constant shifting between spaces, as binaries become blurred and opacities interact. The fragmented texts that make up *Soleil de la conscience* can be read as a series of entries in the author's journal of his first journey to Europe. This cannot be a voyage of discovery in the conventional sense because his colonial education has already made it familiar. So the travel narrative becomes a voyage of self-discovery, for a visitor is both same and other, as he says at the beginning and end of this work, and has "the look of the son and the vision of the outsider."[14] As an outsider the traveler encounters the shock of a sea that is cold, the attraction of the smooth squares of cultivated lands, and the strange foaming beauty of snow. He is as much an insider on the outside as Breton or Mabille in the Caribbean. Indeed, the frequently used image in the text for the perilous negotiations of identity is the agitated sea: "Sensitive

13. St. Aude, "Veillée," *Conjonction* 177–79 (1988), 479.
14. Édouard Glissant, *Soleil de la conscience* (Paris: Seuil, 1957), 19. Page numbers are taken from this edition.

to the to and fro, to the surge of the sea, can I drift on in such a trough between waves, find pleasure or really live there" (11). The illumination that is brought by the emergent sun of consciousness at the end of the journey directly addresses the question of exoticism, which cannot exist in a world that is finite and known, where every traveler is both insider and outsider and every society is same and other. Travel is about the shock of recognition and the subject's self-doubt in the face of the other's light:

> The confrontation of landscapes confirms that of cultures, of sensibilities: not as an exaltation of the Unknown, but as a way of sloughing off a resistant skin in order to understand one's projection in a different light, the shadow of that which we will be. [69]

The relationship of consciousness to matter, location, and reversible space is paramount in this early work, "knowledge comes from matter set free, which turns in on itself, examines itself and falls into place" (10). In the same way that Masson and Breton focus on Diamond Rock in the "Dialogue créole," Glissant projects the cosmopolitan macrocosm of Paris into the luminously opaque monolith of Diamond Rock, thereby provocatively reducing the *métropole* to a kind of open insularity:

> So Paris, in the heart of our time, receives, uproots, blurs, then clarifies and reassures. I suddenly learn its secret: and it is that Paris is an island which draws light from all around and diffracts it immediately. [68]

In this play on "île de France," "ville de lumieres," and "Rocher du Diamant," Glissant deterritorializes Paris, the imagined open insularity of which becomes an exemplary state. Indeed, the island, not as self-contained space but as a zone of encounter and crossing that hardens in the chaos of multiple journeys of wanderings, becomes the key to understanding the dynamics of a cross-cultural world: "The island, which is secret, fulfills itself in its diffused light. Diamond of contradictions as well. . . . The island is a place of passage, what is accumulates lasts" (42).

In the same way that the continental mass must concentrate into cosmopolitan islands, the island-dweller must resist self-exoticizing in relating his grounded reality to the temptation of the "sovereign sea" of history and cross-cultural contact. In a passage that almost seems to write back to Jacques Roumain's novel *Gouverneurs de la rosée* (1944), which, like Césaire's epic poem, evokes the sensory plenitude of his homeland, Glissant destabilizes the temptation of heroic arrivals and grounding centers:

> Strange marriage of earth and heart, under the thrust of the sovereign sea. For here, in the island, the encirclement that risked blocking the imagination on the contrary irritates it and rushes up on it with its chargers from the sea. Then the game is over, the man falls and kisses the earth. . . . Closed in, surrounded, burning to imagine the whole in his image, he must open, open himself, see something else, the other. [22]

The consciousness-raising openness of the island's luminous opacity becomes a dominant motif in an early novel like *La Lézarde* (1958). The relation of center to periphery, of island to sovereign sea is the key to understanding Glissant's first novel. In this narrative of journeys of individual self-discovery during an electoral campaign, Diamond Rock is symbolically featured in the sand bar, created from the opaque deposits of the Lézarde river, with its explosion of foam in the dark sea.

Glissant's poetics of open insularity provides a vision of radical global reordering in which he foresees that "there will no longer be culture without all cultures, no longer civilization that can be the *métropole* of others" (11). These ideas first poetically raised in Glissant's early travel writing in the mid-Fifties results in his first theorizing of relational opacities in the 1969 essay *L'intention poétique* (The Poetic Intention). In this work, Glissant elaborated a theory of dialectical situatedness, a relational model based on density, tension, and contact. "For the poetics of interrelating presupposes that to each one is proposed the density (the opacity) of the other. The more the other resists in his/her density, or fluidity (without being thereby limited), the more his/her reality becomes expressive, and the more fertile the relational encounter."[15] Such a perspective represents, from the 1950s on, an entirely new path for writing for Martinique, Guadeloupe, and Haiti. Indeed, at a time when these places were increasingly isolated from the world around them, because of Departmentalization and Duvalierism, their literature became more enmeshed in the poetics of hemispheric errancy. It is possible to see in the theory of "*réalisme merveilleux*" elaborated by Jacques-Stephen Alexis, René Depestre's association with the Cuban revolution, Glissant's theorization of the Other America, the migrations of Maryse Condé's characters across New World

15. Glissant, *L'intention poétique* (Paris: Gallimard, 1997), 24.

space, and the impossible returns enacted by novelists of the Haitian diaspora, such as Émile Ollivier and Dany Laferrière, manifestations of a poetics of hemispheric relationality that values radical otherness.

Their rupture with what might be termed the Francophone poetics of an earlier generation is tied to the debates of the 1940s in which Breton and Mabille, exiled in the Americas, played central roles. The universalism of Césaire's Negritude, Fanon's national consciousness, or Roumain's Marxism could not be duplicated after World War II. Surrealism in the Caribbean should not be reduced to Jean-Marc Moura's cavalier observation that "it is the primitivism typical of the French Surrealists which has played the role of element of rapprochement with Francophone writers."[16] Such statements simply reinforce notions of a monolingual Francophonie wherein a European center projects modernity onto its linguistic periphery. They repeat the now less than useful limitation of Surrealist poetics to the work of Césaire. They ignore as well the hardening of a radical poetics into the ideology of Negritude with its need to return to authentic cultural sources. They leave out of account the transformation of the Surrealists during their journeys through the Americas and the extent to which the ideas of *"pensée sauvage,"* ethics of opacity, and the new mode of travel writing marked the sensibility of new generations of writers from the Caribbean. The unfortunately marginalized Martinican theorist René Ménil put it clearly in 1959 in the article "De l'exotisme colonial" (Concerning Colonial Exoticism), in which he explains that exoticism is a natural reaction, a palpable but unintelligible presence that recalls Mabille's image of the forest's spreading contours.

> There is an exoticism founded in nature resulting from a particular form of human relation. Finding myself in a foreign land, I am disoriented and perceive the manners, practices, and customs of the native as picturesque and marked with signs of alienness. And as the relation is recriprocal, the native of the land will have a similar, if inverse, vision of me. For him I am as alien as he is for me: he has an exotic vision of me and I have an exotic vision of him. Things cannot be otherwise.[17]

The appeal of a postcolonial poetics of opacity is tied to what Ménil describes as a "normal exoticism" in a world in which cultures have lost their polarity. The Surrealists' insistence on the irreducible

16. Jean-Marc Moura, *Littératures francophones et théorie postcoloniale* (Paris: PUF, 1999), 132.
17. René Ménil, *Tracées* (Paris: Laffont, 1981), 18.

strangeness of things and their capacity to constitute the subject's consciousness is central to this literature, which is about the dynamics of situated opacities. The constant and restless negotiation of dense, specific, resistant space is central to the idea of a poetics of creolization, which is not about hybrid syntheses, but about inventing routes between zones of irreducible difference. By allowing a complicating poetics of opacity to float freely, writers from Haiti, Martinique, and Guadeloupe after the 1950s project a salutary formlessness into the Caribbean imaginary. To simply qualify this writing as "Franco-Antillean," Francophone, or postcolonial, for that matter, misses its central thrust. Caribbean literature from the 1950s on can be fully understood only in terms of the literary transnationalism of the Americas.[18] The dynamics of this new sensibility have been situated by Glissant in the American landscape where "the tiniest, diamantine island poised as if on the brink of imminent eruption"[19] is inextricably tied to a network of paths that wind through a frontier zone of irreducible rocks, where continents fragment into archipelagoes of islands.

18. In her essay "Creolization versus Francophonie," in Maryse Condé, ed., L'héritage de Caliban (Point-à-Pitre: Jasor, 1992), Bernadette Cailler also points to Glissant's importance in theorizing a literature of the Americas outside of francophonie.
19. Glissant, Faulkner, Mississippi (Paris: Stock, 1996), 215.

FRANCESCA CANADÉ SAUTMAN

The Race for Globalization: Modernity, Resistance, and the Unspeakable in Three African Francophone Texts

The "global village" that media pundits and politicians evoke as general currency might well be visualized, in this onset of the twenty-first century, as a village beset by fires, riot, and rampage, where in the stealth of the night one is massacred by neighbors who worship or look differently, or escapes into exile, where hunger reigns unopposed. The paradox of the term poorly conceals the untold violence that the violence of rhetoric seeks to erase. Yet, contemporary African Francophone[1] texts have been tearing off this mask for decades, locating themselves less often in idyllic villages, and more frequently, on the cable lines of suffering between dying villages and indigent cities. In the literature of the 1980s, the focus of this essay, the "village" is already deeply affected by "global economies," but it is hardly a place of intersections, exchange, and communication. Rather, it might be the decaying Congolese village bordered by a cemetery in Tchichelle's "Ilotes et Martyrs"[2]; or the Malian village in Mande Alpha Diarra's *Sahel! sanglante sécheresse*,[3] with its hallucinatory hunger under a brutal regime that steals international aid.[4] Or it could be overcome by famine, banditry, and repression in Moussa Konaté's *Le prix de l'âme*.[5] Or again, it might be perched on sterile Malagasy laterite soil, in Michèle Rakotoson's *Le bain des reliques*.[6] In the war of metaphors, the "*grand village afri-*

1. See my "Hip-Hop/scotch: Sounding Francophone in French and United States Cultures," *France/USA: The Culture Wars, Yale French Studies* 100 (2001): 119–45.
2. Tchichelle Tchivéla, "Ilotes et martyrs," in *Longue est la nuit* (Paris: Hatier, 1980), 82–104; 91.
3. Mande Alpha Diarra, *Sahel! Sanglante sécheresse* (Paris: Présence africaine, 1981).
4. See other texts of the 1980s on hunger: Modibo Sounkalo Keita's *L'archer bassari* (Paris: Karthala, 1984) and Cheikh C. Sow's *Cycle de sécheresse* (Paris: Hatier, 1983)
5. Moussa Konaté, *Le prix de l'âme* (Paris: Présence africaine, 1981).
6. Michèle Rakotoson, *Le bain des reliques*, (Paris: Karthala, 1988).

YFS 103, *French and Francophone*, ed. Farid Laroussi and Christopher L. Miller, © 2003 by Yale University.

cain" evoked by Sylvain Bemba[7] stands at the confluence of the dying village and of the "global village's" pretensions to equitably fuse large and small, rural and urban, local and transnational, indigenous and foreign. And, with millions of Africans on the brink of starvation, politically engaged African writers transform the art of writing as they testify against hunger, political repression, corruption, neocolonialism, genocide, poverty, the condition of women, AIDS, exile, and daily hardship.[8] Their writing is thus an act of resistance against the blandness of postcolonial representations in which all these conditions appear as mere historical accidents. From the 1970s to the present, writers the world over have shared a language of denunciation aimed at neocolonialist and imperialist controls of their cultures and economies. In African texts of the 1980s, that language is noticeably the vector of a descriptive violence that becomes transgressive in its very excess.

Postcolonial theory has deeply modified textual interpretation, questioning the mechanisms of modernity in relation to the "post" world. The reading of Francophone texts must also account for globalization by reaching beyond the postcolonial and incorporating the echoes of resistance to the new world order. The riots of the 1990s in West Africa against the devaluation of the CFA franc, or the placards and gasoline bombs hurled in the streets of Europe and North America at world leaders deciding under heavy protection the fate of entire populations, shadow contemporary, politically engaged literature. African Francophone texts are not transparent palimpsests of the cultures producing them, obliging mirrors of a cultural difference, translated, made palatable and "user friendly" for Western readers. These texts are often painful interrogations of the meaning of modernity—and of postmodernity as well. While seamless accounts of "tradition," colonialism, and postindependence society produce an exonerated version of modernity and reinscribe it into a grand narrative of progress, African Francophone writers make audible and intelligible the sorrow, the clamor, the anger inherent in the competing realities of a continent embattled in what its rulers have anointed the "global world."

7. Sylvain Bemba, *Conversations congolaises,* ed. Alain Brezault and Gérard Clavreuil (Paris: L'Harmattan, 1989), 33.
8. For a panorama of African Francophone literature during the 1980s, see Ambrose Kom, *Dictionnaire des oeuvres littéraires de langue française en Afrique au Sud du Sahara, II 1979–1989* (San Francisco: International Scholars Publications, 1996); and Pius Ngandu Nkashama, *Dictionnaire des oeuvres littéraires africaines de langue française* (Ivry: Éditions Nouvelles du Sud, 1994).

I shall thus discuss three novels, all published in 1988, that are part of a resistant trend in African Francophone writing that emerged as a "new wave" in the 1970s and flourished in the 1980s.[9] These works implode the violence of representation through the violence of enunciation. In them, discursive racial and colonial subjugation is seized and turned around as a weapon aimed at modernist and postmodern complacency. Such texts "write back" to critique and reinterpret Western power structures and to reject the allegedly all-knowing Western gaze.[10]

Michèle Rakotoson's *Le bain des reliques,* Doumbi-Facoly's *Certificat de contrôle anti-sida,*[11] and Yodi Karoné's *Les beaux gosses*[12] were published at a time when the African continent as a whole was reeling from the effects of the world economic recession of the 1980s and when the AIDS pandemic had marked transnational consciousness.[13] Rakotoson evokes famine and the political repression in Madagascar that had just resulted in the deaths of student demonstrators;[14] Karoné addresses urban poverty, violence, and ghettoization in the Ivory Coast in the aftermath of the early 1980s economic crisis.[15] Doumbi-Facoly dares to denounce the phobias elicited by HIV-AIDS.

9. See Madeleine Borgomano, "Linguistic and Cultural Heterogeneity and the Novel in Francophone Africa," in *African Francophone Writing: A Critical Introduction,* ed. Laïla Ibnlfassi and Nicki Hitchcott (Oxford, Washington: Berg, 1996), 125–138. Jonathan Ngate, *Francophone African Fiction: Reading a Literary Tradition* (Trenton, NJ: Africa World Press, 1988), 32–37. Also Pius Ngandu Nkashama *Écritures et discours littéraires: Études sur le roman africain* (Paris: L'Harmattan, 1989), 242–51.

10. Yet, for those who control discourse and the world, says Glissant, it is impossible to give up its "false transparency," to accept merely being in the world, and entering its "penetrable opacity." Édouard Glissant. *Poétique de la relation. Poétique III* (Paris: Gallimard, 1990), 128–29.

11. Doumbi-Facoly, *Certificat de contrôle anti-sida* (Paris: Publisud, 1988).

12. Yodi Karoné, *Les beaux gosses* (Paris: Publisud, 1988). All translations from these three works are my own.

13. See Walter O. Oyugi et al., eds., *Democratic Theory and Practice in Africa* (Portsmouth, NH: Heinemann; London: James Currey, 1988); and Dov Ronen, ed., *Democracy and Pluralism in Africa* (Boulder, Co: Lynne Rienner Publishers, 1986).

14. See Ferdinand Deleris, "De la charte de la Révolution socialiste malagasy aux assises de la francophonie," *Géopolitique africaine* (GA), *Le scandale malgache* (1985): 63–86; "Lettre pastorale des évêques de Madagascar pour le carême 1985," *Ibid,* 87–94. NA, "Bras de fer à Madagascar," *GA* (October 1987): 91–106. Rakotoson, "Instaurer une véritable politique culturelle," *Madagascar: Refondation et développement. Quels enjeux pour les années 2000?,* ed. Patrick Rajoelina (Paris, Montréal: L'Harmattan, 1998), 133–36.

15. See Pascal Koffi Teya, *Côte d'Ivoire. Le roi est nu* (Paris: L'Harmattan, 1985). For Pro-Western views, see Jean-Marc Kalflèche, "Côte d'Ivoire. Le congrès de la consolida-

What connects these works of the late 1980s to globalization? Jo Anne Pemberton suggests that references to the "globe" were common around World War II in arguments for world order, but the term did not become common until after 1960, "referring to a process of worldwide integration" used at the outset "to refer to long-term historical developments as well as a wide range of phenomena," and seen by its proponents as "also a bearer of the new."[16] In 1988, few works in the social sciences or in history evoked the term globalization openly, whereas, since 2000, hundreds of such titles are published in a year. Likewise, in literature, direct responses to globalization are more evident in works of the year 2000 such as Kourouma's *Allah n'est pas obligé*, which denounces the horrors of war in Liberia and Sierra Leone, international indifference, and the destructive intervention of the ECOMOG forces. Or Mongo Beti's *Branle-bas en blanc et noir*, which announces the ethnic clashes of the Ivory Coast and Cameroon, between North and South, Muslim and Christian/animist. Yet, writing from the late eighties does embody—literally, since it inscribes suffering, abject bodies in texts—a poetics of denunciation and resistance to the "global world." This is an important moment in African Francophone literature: the violence of representation reappropriated by former colonial subjects in an act of literary agency complicates postindependence denunciations of homegrown dictatorships and of foreign intervention, often within a Marxist framework. In the 1980s, these texts already acknowledged that many aspects of today's world *are* global, while formulating a resistant discourse on mass poverty and war that is not ascribed to the actions of a single Western power, but to the global West, for which the present USA often acts as a "stand-in." This poetics, which often makes the body central to its representational strategies, leads me to theorize resistance at least in part as giving voice to the unspeakable.

Globalization will thus be treated as a phenomenon overlapping with but distinct from imperialism, whose main characteristics are the interconnectedness of media, culture, and police and information services; massive transnational conglomerates and free trade operating to their advantage; international intervention in local conflicts; the ex-

tion," *GA* (March 1986): 113–120, and Yves Catalans, "Côte d'Ivoire. La continuité a triomphé de la crise," Ibid., 121–132.

16. Jo Anne Pemberton, *Global Metaphors: Modernity and the Quest for one World* (London, Sterling Va.: Pluto Press, 2001), 154.

pansion of racial boundaries, simultaneous with increased ethnic warfare; the impact of pandemics such as AIDS on international and national policy, linked in part to the numbers infected but also to the cultural implications of its means of transmission. These elements are paralleled by world-wide tensions around uniformization of cultural products and social custom, and linguistic dominance, countered by renewed fervor for national and local languages, and the careful manipulation of tradition.[17] Occupation of space, the role of locality and place, as Saskia Sassen has remarked, are crucial correctives to globalization, allowing agency to marginalized peoples.[18]

The "global" world also produces a transnational postmodern text, often written in exile, or uprooted, or even eschewing all roots.[19] Thus, Rakotoson's text, written in France, addresses ethnic clashes and historical scars in Madagascar. Karoné, a Cameroonian, chose to write about the Ivory Coast and its quasi-mythical city, Abidjan, filled with immigrants from Burkina-Faso, Ghana, and the Sahel. Finally, Doumbi-Facoly, a Malian living in Senegal, placed his novel of AIDS discrimination in a recognizable France and left the African nation at stake unnamed. All three novels also adopt traits of the mystery novel, a genre given to spatial uncertainties and identity breakdowns. While the characters are not detectives, they struggle desperately to find out the truth before it kills them, possibly the very truth that will kill them: such is the case of Ranja, Kairuane, and the mother-daughter couple in *Certificat*. Thus both nation and truth are uprooted and shifted into dangerous waters, where textuality gives substance to fluid, unstable realities.

Such texts also exemplify a current in African Francophone writing of the last decades that makes the *unspeakable* readable. This refers not merely to something that is impossible or extremely difficult to "say," but further, to utter; it is connected to voice, not merely to communication. In the word "unspeakable," in English, there is also a subjective notion of that which cannot/should not be spoken because it is indecent, scandalous, morally repugnant, as in "unspeakable acts." It

17. See Célestin Monga, *Anthropologie de la colère: Société civile et démocratie en Afrique* (Paris: L'Harmattan, 1994), 30–50.

18. Saskia Sassen, *Globalization and its Discontents* (New York: The New Press, 1998), introduction, esp. xxi.

19. See Mongo Beti, "L'exil après l'exil?" *Peuples noirs, peuples africains* [*PNPA*] 14.80 (March–April 1991): 110-25. Azadé Seyhan, *Writing Outside the Nation* (Princeton and Oxford: Princeton University Press, 2001).

inscribes violence in the word because it forces to speak that which should remain silenced, against one's wishes or against censorship. *Unspeakable* reaches beyond conceptualization, grapples with making known what is already there but hidden, and seeks spaces of enunciation unencumbered by previous modes of discourse.

The power of neocolonialism and imperialism can thus only be matched by the textual resistance of voicing the "unspeakable." Such texts effectively displace the remnants of discourse bequeathed by modernity by the use of enunciatory resistance: gruesome acts of violence and relentless economic oppression are not merely described as elicited by African actors, but are shown in a context where non-Africans operate freely as communities or as tentacular economic powers. What Homi Bhabha calls the "disjunctive temporalities of modernity,"[20] are expressed in the narrative mode of disarray (as in Tchichelle's 1980 short stories, and in Karoné's and Doumbi-Facoly's breathless narrative style) and by a fierce identification of lack, inequity, and violence. Speaking the unspeakable reflects Bhabha's "locus and locution of cultures caught in the transitional and disjunctive temporalities of modernity."[21]

The novels I discuss here are representative of a wide current in African writing that refuses to quietly acquiesce to a "postcolonial condition." For Guy Ossito Midiohouan, postindependence writing, especially since 1970, has yielded a specifically Black African novel, with "a systematic strategy of transgression . . . [and] a rebel imagination."[22] What some political analysts have termed "patrimonial authoritarianism" in all the regimes of Francophone Africa that came to power in the 1970s, has been made possible, according to Achille Mbembe, by an entire culture of the "postcolony." This postcolony is at once a political regime and a culture, "to some extent deprived of references to face modernity and delivered to . . . sex, the belly, and the sacred."[23] In

20. Homi K. Bhabha, *The Location of Culture*, (New York and London: Routledge, 1994), 250–51.

21. The notion of the unspeakable is useful as well in reading other novels of the eighties. See Ibrahima Ly's *Toiles d'araignées*, (Paris: L'Harmattan, 1982), a terrifying account of incarceration in Beleya prison. In *La retraite anticipée du Guide Suprême* (Paris: L'Harmattan, 1989), Doumbi-Facoly evokes the torture of political prisoners as acts that, because they are too horrific to witness, must be reconstituted by sound and remain as visible traces in the bruising and cutting of lips (160–67).

22. Guy Ossito Midiohouan, *L'utopie négative d'Alioum Fantouré. Essai sur le Cercle des Tropiques* (Paris: Silex, 1984), 12–16.

23. Alain Ricard, "La libération de la parole en Afrique francophone 1989–1992,"

effect, Rakotoson, Karone, and Doumbi-Facoly undermine and distance the very notion of postcolony through three complex "denunciatory" novels that are written against an odious, at times occult,
encroaching global reality. Yet, none of these three novels blandly embraces "tradition" as an antidote to the brutalities of modernity; rather,
echoing V. Y. Mudimbe's rejection of modernity and tradition as a suspect dichotomy,[24] they question global agendas and the deep scarring
left by modernity, while taking a critical look at "tradition's" changing
and multifarious role.

LE BAIN DE RELIQUES

In Rakotoson's novel, a journalist from the city is invited to film an ancient ceremony, a sacred ritual of Malagasy royalty in a forlorn region,
the Mid-West. The motives of his employer and the politicians who organize the filming are suspect, and he discovers fragments of an oppressive reality filled with starvation and political massacres. But he
cannot complete his work, for he is killed in mysterious conditions, after a tryst with the local warlord's woman.

Bain strongly bears out Homi Bhabha's notion of "distanciating."
Underlining Fanon's role in opposition to an ontology of Black man's
"belatedness," Bhabha advocates writing that does not merely contra-
dict "the metaphysical idea of progress or racism or rationality," but
"distanciates them," "making them uncanny by displacing them in a
number of culturally contradictory and discursively estranged loca-
tions" (36–37). As we shall see, this process is at work in *Bain*. Further,
if modernity is, as Appadurai has suggested, inseparable from a dominant narrative of historical origin (2–3) based on racial hierarchies, it
reveals its own vulnerability. In an uncompromising interrogation of
the defining historical moment of independence, African Francophone
writers such as Rakotoson unsettle the continuities and hierarchies of
modernity's complacent colonial world; they rescue submerged blocks
of history, of discourse, of memory. In *Bain*, a voice rises through the
narrative collusion of oral and written, fragile but undaunted. The
past—the ancestral ceremony of royal relics—is inscribed in the very
first pages, the prologue, with the repetition of the formula "once upon

---

Afriques imaginaires. Regards réciproques et discours littéraires 17e–20e, ed. Anny
Wynchank and Philippe-Joseph Salazar (Paris: L'Harmattan, 1995), 281–95; 293.
    24. V. I Mudimbe, *The Invention of Africa* (Bloomington and Indianapolis: Indiana
University Press, 1988), 189, 197.

a time there was the ceremony" (7–8), an incantation or prescriptive enunciation against forgetting, against the quiet acquiescence to the global culture that will follow in the next pages, which describe the city. That past is then distanced to another region, with a strange, barren landscape, another set of geopolitical contours, creating an almost "ethnological" inserting of the ancestral ritual that then turns inward, against its observers, although they are Malagasy as well. Finally, it is the strangeness of film in a place so isolated and bereft of basic survival needs, its anachronic disjuncture with both the ceremony and the place itself, combined with the irrelevance of "rationality" in the ceremonial proceedings, that effect that distancing.

Ethnic tensions within one nation are an important sub-theme of *Le bain des reliques*. All the protagonists are Malagasy, but there are strong differences between the people of the coasts and those of the high plateaus, as well as underlying Black/White dichotomies. The street children and beggars are called *andevo* (son of a slave), "the woe of those born a little darker, a little curlier" (21). Government massacres of villagers, with hundreds, sometimes thousands, of bodies piling up and rotting in the sun cement a deep estrangement between ethnic groups and city versus rural regions. The villagers refer to the film crew members from the city as "from the white men's land," "foreigner, white man" (7, 51). City dwellers are considered richer, more modern, and thus in collusion with oligarchy and imperialism; the villagers are poorer but somehow nobler, less tainted (73–83). Thus the hero at once disdains their ways (24) and feels inferior with respect to caste and race (51, 53, 56); he marvels that "he, the man from the high plateaus, the *mavo ranjo*, the man with the sallow calves, the pale man of the sunless hills, the man from the hated ethnic group, would be allowed to film, tell, record, preserve" (29).

In *Bain*, Antananarivo is a dreary, indigent city inhabited by desperate bands of abandoned children who live off theft and are kept in line through mutilations by the militia and their own street hierarchy (18–20, 24). Urban banditry had become a major social question in Madagascar in the 1980s, and it had ethnic and racial dimensions. In contrast to the deprivation experienced by the many, the global world leaves its traces in the form of money and consumer goods—French pastry shops, US soft drinks, and the World Bank. Such textual markers reflect disillusion with Western economic promises, resentment of dependency, anxiety at cultural homogenization, and resistance to the role of US-controlled financial institutions in African economies.

LES BEAUX GOSSES

Kairuane's real father is a marginalized dancer, and his mother is a has-been musician and a drug addict. However, he thinks he is the son of a powerful gangster, who raised him in luxury, after inflicting crippling injuries on the dancer in a fight. When the gangster is murdered, Kairuane falls into the spiraling heel of economic deprivation, petty crime, and deception. He is finally executed by his acolytes after murdering his real father.

Like *Bain*, *Les beaux gosses* complicates ethnic and national scripts, here through the presence of the rich Lebanese community, culturally different but invested with a considerable amount of power, who commandeer part of the underworld and work in collusion with local powers. Implicit in the novel is the question of citizenship and nationality, central in later Ivory Coast politics: indeed, "ivoirité" provoked riots with the results of the March 2002 elections.

Abidjan, the setting of *Les beaux gosses*, is an international site, teeming with poverty and crime, whose inhabitants develop strategies of economic and cultural survival similar to those of modern American ghettoes and French urban zones.[25] And "Les beaux gosses" ["beautiful kids"] is not, as one might surmise, a nickname for delinquent youth, but a sumptuous villa, surrounded by lavish gardens, and situated high up on a hill, yet still close to Treichtown, the slum. The villa, even abandoned, and the urban topography—hill, lagoon, slums, coastline—are the locus of fantasies and hopes, and underdevelopment is the hidden face of a blatant overdevelopment characterized by brash consumerism. In the novel, urban crime becomes a site of potential resistance to the cynical efficiency of official power, incarnated here by the coalition of the Ivorian political class and the rich Lebanese. References to the Black American city are very ambiguous: the fresco depicting "Harlem the negress" is painted on the jail wall with shoe polish, paint, chalk, and even blood by the professional killer Mobio. It features, over Harlem, the severed hand of the Statue of Liberty, an Arabian stallion prancing in front of a limousine draped in the US flag, a boxer watch-

25. The stark film *Bronx-Barbès* (2000) depicts street youth in Abidjan. Dir. Eliane de Latour, scr. Emmanuel Bourdieu and Eliane de Latour. On Abidjan: Alain Bonnaissieux, *L'autre Abidjan. Chronique d' un quartier oublié* (Abidjan: Inades; Paris: Karthla, 1987); Philippe Haeringer, *Abidjan au coin de la rue. Éléments de la vie citadine dans la métropole ivoirienne* (Paris: Cahiers ORSTOM, Série sciences humaines, 1983, 19/4).

ing Marilyn Monroe falling down the Empire State Building, and a black child who has placed his head on his skateboard to listen to a sermon by the Reverend Jesse Jackson, crucified on a cement cross (32). Mobio claims to be an "American," rotting by mistake in this Ivorian jail: he subscribes to a revisionist version of slavery, admonishing his pupil to not believe "all that nonsense they tell about slaves." In his own counternarrative, women and ancient African history are stepping stones to male agency: his ancestor, he claims, sold his three wives to gain passage on the boat, then impregnated a "Malinke lady" on-board and "reached the promised land" together with her (39). Mobio, paid to enforce the underworld criminal order of the Lebanese businessmen, dreams of going to the USA, but to kill people for more money. In his words, the American dream has become the American nightmare. Americans, he adds, love death "with napalm, chain saws, electricity," because of the "Indians, the Secession War, the Mafia, Vietnam . . . " (41).

The "reverse rooting" of African Francophone texts in African-American literature in diasporic and transnational counter-roots usually links unsettling notions of "race" to African postcolonial identities and disjunctive interventions in the "violence of representation." But, in the postmodern, postcolonial context the mythical nature of America/the USA/New York bequeathed by modernity has shifted dramatically,[26] as it does in Karoné's novel: Black America has lost some of its salvific value and become part of America the globalizer.

Karoné's novel also underscores the tensions between hybridity and globalization. Half African, Julie Madola is a talented musician, but her musical genius and the musical culture she represents are devalued, even silenced. When she and the dancer try a comeback, Julie's previous fame draws a crowd that does not, however, understand her music. She refuses to play the bland cocktail lounge jazz they are accustomed to, turns her back on the audience, and plays discordant, disdainful notes on her sax, which becomes her true voice and mouth, freed and regenerated from its previous confinement to sexual subjection and humiliation under the gangster's rule. Only her fellow musicians, including an American from the Bronx, understand the despair and re-

26. See Guy Rossatanga-Rignault, "Vieilles lunes et nouveaux empires. Un regard africain sur la France et les Etats-Unis," *Afrique, la fin du Bas Empire, LiMes. Revue française de géopolitique* 3 (1997): 67–79.

bellion she is sounding to the very end of her music. The fiasco is a reflection on the tyranny of global culture. Julie's Afro-Caribbean jazz is unpalatable to these West African consumers, who, like the gangster, do not see jazz "as they do in America as a liberating music" (58). In contrast, "Summertime," played by popular demand, encodes racial and global hierarchies. For Julie and the musicians, it has no meaning, no soul. It is a piece of commercially safe, made by/for whites, fake "black sound" (130–38). "Summertime" signals the global media's project of promoting rigid and normative blocks of identity, of erasing true hybridity, and quashing resistant voices. Jazz is a central language in this work: a bridge, but also a terrain of cultural contestation.[27] On a deep allegorical level, in contrast to the corruption of the visible signaled by Mobio's fresco, jazz effectuates a reverse migration from the displaced roots of the African Diaspora culture. It is true Black sound/ soul, and the language of resistance, struggling to be heard and valorized, even in Africa. The ill-starred dancer's own hybrid art loses the battle against the global market as he interprets a traditional Senufo epic in a work that combines African dances, ballet, and even break-dancing, only to be reviled by the audience. The Senufo are a rich Ivorian code in the text; their misuse as tourist attractions, their poverty in the marginalized North, their political opposition to Houphouët-Boigny's dictatorial regime,[28] as well as the reference to their cultural traditions, are all traces of the local in its struggle against global uniformity. This performance stands in stark contrast to the very last scene, where the authorities have offered a free concert to the masses, and successfully peddle local and national patriotism along with commercial pop versions of world music (177–79).

CERTIFICAT DE CONTRÔLE ANTI-SIDA

Certificat details the systematic destruction of a biracial family. The African father, a political opponent of an unidentified regime, is accused of carrying AIDS and detained in Africa, incommunicado. His French wife and their daughter try to free him; they are subjected to discrimination and violence, and betrayed by the wife's own racist French

27. Zora Neale Hurston wrote of jazz, warriors, and jungles in "How It Feels to Be Colored Me," *World Tomorrow* 11 (May 1928): 215–16.
28. Georges Coffy, *Le soleil des exclus. Côte d'Ivoire. La lutte pour la démocratie.* (Paris: La pensée universelle, 1994). On Lauren Gbagbo in Senufo country, see 69–85.

father; finally they are incarcerated in Europe and commit suicide. *Certificat* denounces collective psychosis and its collusion with the state and public institutions in response to AIDS in the West and in Africa.

Fear of contamination leads the "modern" Western world to repression and atavism. Science implodes and racial reasoning takes hold as a coalition of scientists pins the origin of the disease on Africa and in particular on alleged sexual practices with the green monkey. Racial hegemony is enshrined in the exoneration of everyone except Africans, not even defended by their own governments (59–67). In the face of virulent racial suspicion and even attacks, Africans in the West hide and deny their identity. Doumbi-Facoly's sardonic pen takes a Fanonian look[29] at various practices of surgical modification that amount to mutilation and can end tragically: one man hates his nose, a woman her buttocks. And many try to pass as members of the "higher" echelon in the racial hierarchy, as Black Americans or Caribbeans (70–77), whose position shifts imperceptibly from liberationist to collusionist. In this grinding but quintessentially postcolonial tragedy, the child has to be the narrator, because as a *métisse* she is a cipher and mediator of racial conflict. The *métisse* is not merely a critical reflection on the impossibility of colonial rule, as s/he could be in earlier novels, but signals the preposterous nature of racial classifications, an interpellation of normative discourse about race. In *Certificat*, distancing operates through an Afrocentric dream sequence linked to ancestral, familial, and village soothsaying traditions and a syncretic religious vision that reclaims Egyptian gods, refusing Western readings of African history that have "disappeared" ancient Egypt from the continent.

Doumbi-Facoly's *Certificat* paints another type of city: a Western location—most probably Paris—ruled by the laws, discrimination, and violence of "good" citizens. In this city, where the doors of justice close in the two women's face, there is a counter-city, made of African and Caribbean community networks that are called to the rescue. These include the slightly dubious but perfectly accurate African diviner, and the mysterious "Tonton," an elusive character in keeping with the detective/mystery aspect of the work, with contacts on both sides of the cultural and power divide. This is the global contemporary city of the West, whose fractured whiteness is constantly challenged and is linked

29. See Frantz Fanon's denunciation of self-hating mechanisms in his 1952 classic, *Black Skin, White Masks,* trans. Charles Lam Markmann (New York: Grove Press, 1967).

by myriad threads to the rest of the world. Globalism is an important subtheme of the novel, since the AIDS crisis itself invokes international responses, or the lack thereof. The narrative of loss and destruction is completed when the two women try to escape with Tonton's help, and reach another European country en route to Africa. Their plane is hijacked by Palestinians and, in the ensuing shoot-out, all passengers are grounded; mother and daughter are caught and forcibly returned. In the mode of disaster and the absurd, Doumbi-Facoly has carefully inscribed a global world where all conflicts end up interconnected and cumulatively affect their victims, identified by their special interracial bonds. Space has an important function in this representation: the village of the father, albeit unnamed, remains a locus of desire and hope, while global spaces such as airports and planes are charged with menacing violence. The virtual space of the child's dream sequence and the suspended one of their attempted flight momentarily abolish the spaces of the global order and propose a counter-globality devoid of oppressive systems.

UN/SPEAKING GLOBAL

In the end, through ambiguous uses of French, the unspeakable surfaces and takes form in the three novels analyzed here, as it does in other works of the 1980s. In *Bain*, it surfaces through Ranja's death, which remains clouded in mystery: does this death result from a mere conflict of passion, from a sexual insult and breach of propriety? Was it an accident or a suicide? Or was it a sacrificial offering with Ranja as an unknowing scapegoat? Or again, was he assassinated for his political views by his very collaborators? Silence falls on his death, marked by the unopened, unreturned letters from his wife, while the cameraman attempts to make sense of the deed, the film, and the fragments of Ranja's life. In *Les beaux gosses*, the unspeakable is linked to the classical Freudian scene—the brutal murder of the father by the (unknowing) son. The son's incestuous leanings toward his mother explode in her barely whispered revelation of the true crime. When Kairuane is gruesomely hacked to pieces by his former acolytes, the membra disjecta of his unformed identity and speech lie in a garbage can near the road. Finally, in *Certificat*, the unspeakable vibrates in the treason committed by the racist and colonialist father; he falsifies his own daughter's health certificate, leading to her being fired, hounded, and jailed for fleeing the country. The only possible response to such an act is the simultaneous suicide of mother and daughter, who, separated by walls, join to nullify speech itself by ending the narrative of betrayal, and voiding the utterance of triumph over their bodies. Violence makes the unspeakable known and denunciatory: the mother cuts her veins, an echo of the accusation of tainted blood against the husband, and the child seeks exile through death to the land of ancestors, an echo of the father's exile in a no man's land. All in all, in these three texts, resistance to the effects of the global world order has been effectuated through overcoming the unspeakable and through the enunciation of violent acts.

Jonathan Ngate has remarked that Paul Bamboté's *Princesse Mandapu* (1972), a novel that is foundational in its very singularity, belonged "to a small group of literary African Francophone texts that, since the seventies, broadcast their autonomy, if not their independence, towards French literature," through including and excluding African or other partners in the "workings of their discourse." He adds, "it is quite possible that the French language has become, in these texts, the locus of a separation that reveals the other face of the realm, close but distant, and lets other voices be heard."[30]

The global world with which contemporary African literature is contending seems to leave a shrinking place for *Francophonie*. French must share the stage with other non-African languages: as a sacred language, the vector of faith to many millions of Africans, Arabic maintains a special status. As a language perceived, rightly or wrongly, as the vector of economic development, English has been encroaching steadily.[31] English can signal the nefarious effects of US interests in the African continent, or open forms of oppositional discourse of African diasporic roots and Blackness. That position by itself confers to it a powerful role as linguistic shadow and crossing. The global also means that "African solutions"—a term used by historian Basil Davidson in speaking of ancient Africa—imply the inscription of African partners, African interlocutors, and African intertextuality in works of literature, as Ngate suggested. Further, in a variety of initiatives of the last

30. Jonathan Ngate, *"Princesse Mandapu,"* PNPA, 9.53/54 (September–December 1986): 184–90; 186.
31. On violent conflicts between the Francophone and Anglophone communities in Cameroon: Mongo Beti, "Cameroun. La deuxième guerre civile a-t-elle commencé?" PNPA 8/48 (November–December 1985): 1–6, and, in the same volume, "Lettre ouverte à tous les parents Anglophones," which is signed, simply, "Étudiants anglophones": 7–20.

few decades, texts in African languages have been published.[32] Some of the very same African authors who write in French, like Michèle Rakotoson, are writing and have been writing, in their own African language/s. Other writers implode the purity of French through the use of *moussa*.[33] Others again, like Doumbi-Facoly,[34] inveigh virulently against *Francophonie* while writing in French. All of this bodes ill for Francophone exclusivity, and even more so, for the ideological hegemony of *Francophonie*.

Witness to that opposition is the journal founded by Mongo Beti, entitled *Peuples noirs, peuples africains*, which, from 1985 to 1991, published a series of vitriolic essays against the role of France in Africa and the function of *Francophonie*. These were mostly penned by Mongo Beti and Guy Ossito Midiohouan, with such titles as "Le degré zéro de la décolonisation," "Tiens! Revoilà les tirailleurs sénégalais," "Seigneur, délivre-nous de la francophonie," and "Un sottisier francophone."[35] All of this was written in French, an indication of how wide the gulf is between the linguistic use of French and the political content of *Francophonie* as an institution.

Yet, the sheer volume of literary works being produced in French from outside the Hexagon clearly indicates that Francophone writing is not about to disappear, even if the relationship with the font of that language, France, remains volatile. And regardless of the bitter criticism of France and its role, the leaden weight of US power in matters of international affairs and global economy[36] engenders other forms of opposition, as virulent or moreso. In the vortex created by resistance to the role of the United States, especially in the first decade of the twenty-first century, and especially in relation to the exploding Middle East,

32. Pierre Medehouegnon, "'Lò ou l'offensive africaine contre la francophonie?" *PNPA* 8/45 (September–October 1985): 120–22 [collection of proverbs in Fon].

33. See Koffi Kwahulé, *Pour une critique du théâtre ivoirien* (Paris: L'Harmattan, 1996), 208–10. *Moussa* is a form of phonetic and broken-down French spoken by Africans in subaltern positions under the French colonial administration and seen by the French as a mark of ridicule, but turned around by African Francophone writers as an implicit resistance to the French language and the politics of linguistic "purity."

34. Doumbi-Facoly, *Guide*, 30–34; 138–39; 196–97.

35. See Guy Ossito Midiohouan, Mongo Beti, and Max Liniger-Goumaz, "Deux ou trois choses sur 'Jeune Afrique,'" *PNPA* 8/44 (March–April 1985): 11–34. See, in the same volume, Beti, "Conseils à un jeune écrivain francophone": 52–60.

36. See Denis Bra Kanon (Minister of Agriculture of the Ivory Coast), "Matières premières. Oui au libéralisme, non à l'injustice," *Géopolitique africaine* (June 1986): 21–26.

there is still a great margin of maneuver for the concept of Franco-phonie. Globalization is also marked by below-surface tensions among local and regional language, even in Europe, demanding their due, and underscoring the fragility of the artificial power of both English and French.

In sum, the study of African Francophone literature has been, for too long, streamlined into Western and conservative canons and expectations. As Guy Midiohouan suggested, not reading beyond the 1960s produces a skewed, ideologically safe perception of this literature. The last two decades in particular have produced a wealth of works that are at once intricate and at times revolutionary, examples of the writer's craft, and complex sites of multiple contestations, rejecting a global world order deleterious to Africans. Within this moment, the writing of the 1980s is crucial to the genealogy of denunciatory African Fran-cophone literature, and the three novels discussed here are highly rep-resentative of these currents. All three writers deftly wove the numer-ous social, cultural, and political conflicts in their country or region into the denunciatory strategies of the novel: for Rakotoson, it was the massive poverty, glorious historical past, colonial and internal politi-cal violence of Madagascar. Narrative riddles remain unsolved, and a character marked by sexual and gender ambiguity, the cameraman, must see in lieu of Ranja and complete the filming in the midst of a pageantry of political recuperation. Karoné evoked the violence and de-privation of sprawling modern West African cities, palimpsests of sim-ilar conditions in the West, and in particular the powerful USA, thus exposing the latter's fragility along with African realities that include questioning current national/nationalist parameters. Thus, the final celebration of state power run by a multicultural group of exploiters was spoiled by the preceding portrayal of a grieving Julie, having buried the *men* in her life, slowly proceeding to create her own life *ambitus:* self-loving gestures, light and bright colors, song, renewed maternity. Doumbi-Facoly took Western nations, represented by France, and despotic African regimes to the mat for their ferocious reactions to and political manipulations of HIV-AIDS. He also conferred the last words of resistance on a trio of women—the grandmother informs the absent "Monsieur le Président" that both her daughter and grand-daughter took their own lives—who refuse silence and oppression through sui-cide and the maternal genealogy.

In the end, all three novels denounced a wide range of social and political ills, and resisted their own pessimistic conclusions in scenes that appear to reiterate the power of hegemonic forces, as they undermine it through characters who occupied marginalized and/or subjected positions. Through a dis/embodied poetics of violence, these novels have shattered the consensual foundations of the global, wielding the trenchant weapon of the disenfranchised, the subaltern, the "peripheral," dissent that can return the "unspeakable" to speech and finally to writing.[37]

37. The most apt metaphor for this process can be found in Karonés last pages: "Forgotten jazz woman who errs among the graves . . . torrid shadow chased by a spear of light, Julie Madola eats earth every time. And contrary to popular belief, the earth of the dead has a slight taste of freedom . . ." (175).

MIREILLE ROSELLO

Unhoming Francophone Studies: A House in the Middle of the Current

I cannot separate my individual practice from the field of academic study known as "Francophone studies" nor from the type of institution that asks me to represent the label. It is one of the difficulties that I accept without too much anxiety. I cannot ignore the existence of the category, and yet, the relationship between my professional activities and that abstract object (of desire, of fear?) is far from clear: I am obviously not writing as a "representative" of a particular constituency of Francophone specialists (no one mandates me). On the other hand, my interest in Caribbean literature or in Algerian history has forced me, and allowed others, to use a label that institutional convention has legitimized. I consider myself a happy yet recalcitrant Francophonist.

MONSIEUR OU MADAME JOURDAIN

Like Molière's character, I may have always "done" Francophone studies without knowing it, but deciding whether what I do, can, must, or should (not) be called "Francophone studies" changes everything. When I read Alexandre Dumas in my *lycée* in France, in the 1960s, was his ethnicity ever discussed? Of course not. When we studied Saint-John Perse's *Éloges* did I ever ask myself where the poet came from?[1] No, he was a "French poet." Did I, as a result, experience a sense of discomfort and frustration? I did not, nor was I encouraged to ask if others did. I did not even know what I was excluding. The question "where does the poet come from?" was unthinkable.[2] Today, I would not teach

1. See Saint-John Perse, *Éloges* (Paris, Gallimard, 1960).
2. Not that the truth about Saint-John Perse has been restored once it is said that he is from Guadeloupe: an asymmetry persists between the time when it was easy to "naturalize" Henri Michaux, Samuel Beckett, and Saint-John Perse and our present when the

YFS 103, *French and Francophone,* ed. Farid Laroussi and Christopher L. Miller, © 2003 by Yale University.

123

the same authors without at least raising the issues of Dumas's hybridity and of Saint-John Perse's *créolité*.

I should add, however, that I have no desire to blame my high school teachers for their methods or choices. They operated at the crossroads between a genuine commitment to literature and national programmatic necessity. In 1973, Aimé Césaire was not part of our course on Surrealism, and no one helped me discover Senegalese novelists or the idea of non-Hexagonal French literature. Yet, in their own way, my teachers of French were dissidents and I am grateful to them for nurturing my interest in literature and literary criticism (even if "explications de texte" did seem a bit artificial) at a time when being a "good student" meant opting for the sciences. They did not help me discover the definition of a literary canon, of its national and international politics (perhaps they actually believed that they were teaching us French Literature rather than creating, through their teaching, a nationally uniform set of literary references). They did, however, make me aware that disciplines had something to do with power, that they could be in a position of rivalry. They taught me that "literature" as a whole was a contested field: the gradual legitimization of French cultural studies in recent years would only confirm their lessons.

That original doubt as to the intrinsic value of the Humanities (an uncertainty that previous generations may not have experienced) never disappeared and probably explains why I never tried to invest in a (provisionally) triumphant or at least dominant disciplinary model. Today, I don't think that my own teaching is authorized or validated by my adherence to some sort of official code called "Francophone studies" even if it is now possible to be hired under that umbrella. Francophone studies is a performative statement that may or may not be useful ten years from now.

Consequently, on the one hand, the idea that I might have to determine who belongs to which field, to police necessarily porous border, to assess who is a marginal and who is a full-fledged citizen of that territory generates in me a case of instant mental fatigue. Is it ludicrous for a Rousseau specialist to present herself as a Francophone studies expert? Theoretically speaking, I do not know. If only one "Francophone" course is offered in the catalogue, it may be cynical and opportunistic

---

poet's "problematic belonging" becomes the object of inquiry, as Régis Antoine puts it in *La littéature franco-antillaise. Haïti, Guadeloupe et Martinique* (Paris: Khartala, 1992), 293.

to devote it to Rousseau and his "Swissitude." It may be intellectually and politically interesting (as well) were the relationship between the content of the course and the idea of Francophone studies treated with rigor and integrity. Would I do it? If only one course were offered, I would probably concentrate on two simultaneous goals: I would try to present students with samples from my own areas of expertise (Guadeloupean or Moroccan novelists, Francophone revolutionary poetry from the 1950s), and also make them aware of how the course was structured, of what type of institutional constraints allowed its existence and limited its potentially subversive material. I would suggest that they interrogate the issues privileged by the syllabus (creolization, marginalization and periphery, the historical link between a *métropole* and its previously colonized satellites, the contemporary manifestations of literary bad faith and editorial lip service). In other words, I would not start from a definition of Francophone studies, but, rather, would ask students to tell me what definition they thought I proposed.

On the other hand, we *are* constantly policing the territory: practical, tactical, historical, and financial reasons lead us to choose. We select courses, authors, programs; we decide which colleagues get tenure; we help to choose which books get published, which rejected. And in those cases, mental fatigue is not a powerful political tool: but there is room for maneuver[3] between the inertia of departmental Pax Romana (that tends to favor a self-perpetuating definition of what is good and always was) and full-blown disciplinary wars, with colleagues defending what their enemies call their "empire."

A HOUSE IN THE MIDDLE OF THE CURRENT

When our postcolonial Monsieur Jourdain seeks to formulate a theoretical and historical model of "Francophone studies," that (hybrid and androgynous) allegorical figure always ends up in what Michel Serres calls the "third" space, the middle of the river, the vortex that any migrant discovers after leaving the native land and before reaching the new shore.[4] The idea of "Francophone studies" is not the name of a new border but a turbulence that creates distance between different pedagogical territories: how can I research and teach my interest in "French" or in France or in the relationship between the two? French as an in-

---

3. See Ross Chambers, *Room for Maneuver* (Chicago: Chicago University Press, 1993).

4. Michel Serres, *Le tiers instruit* (Paris: François Bourin, 1991).

ternational language cannot be equated with national borders but no one can deny that it has historically been fused with a triumphant celebration of France. Is it strategically effective to "simply" concentrate on literary, cultural, or political texts produced *in* French, or in any one of the nations that counts French as one of its languages? Each decision imposes a back and forth between academic and intellectual territories, between history and literature, anthropology and the history of anthropology, linguistics and language acquisition, and while the institutions where we teach or learn probably prefer the solidification of the field, each scholar and student's research will remain in the middle of the river.

> We do not, we cannot live on this fault line, on this axis, on this whirlpool: who would build a house in the middle of the current? No institution, no system, no science, no language, no gesture, no thought is not founded on this mobility. Which is the ultimate foundation and founds nothing.
>
> We can only move in its direction, but when we are about to reach it, we leave it, driven by the forces that move away from it. We only spend there one infinitesimal moment. The time and space of extreme concentration. [Serres, 55; my translation]

This is the "time-and-space" of a university course or research project, where one type of intersection of or tangential lines between definitions can be studied.

For the purpose of one experiment, I could choose to focus on the relationship between genre, language, and the national. I would provisionally feign a certain indifference to the issue of national linguistic politics and teach a course on "le roman policier," or detective novel. The reading list would include George Simenon's novels and Patrice Leconte's cinematographic adaptations, as well as Driss Chraïbi's *L'inspecteur Ali à Trinity College*,[5] Hubert Aquin's *Prochain épisode*,[6] and Anne Garréta's *La décomposition*.[7] Here, the challenge would be to define what type of encounter such a list created between France, Belgium, Quebec, and Morocco, but also England or Switzerland.

Or, remembering my second confluent where "Francophone studies" connects literatures historically brought together by colonization, I could offer a course that focuses on the ambivalence of linguistic pol-

5. Driss Chraïbi, *L'inspecteur Ali à Trinity College* (Paris: Denoël, 1996).
6. Hubert Aquin, *Prochain épisode* (Paris: Laffont, 1966).
7. Anne Garréta, *La décomposition* (Paris: Grasset, 1999).

itics and on the parallel that can be established with the students' personal experience of language acquisition. The corpus would change significantly: I would point out to my students that most Francophone authors have written *about* their relationship to the French language and
that they could therefore learn about their own form of multilinguil-
ism by studying the (often metaphorical) models Francophone authors
develop in their texts. For Assia Djebar's *L'amour la fantasia*,[8] the
French language is "embrasure" (147) [window to the world], but also
"langue marâtre" (244) [a mean stepmother of a language] or the "tu-
nique de Nessus" (243) [Nesssus's tunic], while the unwritten native
language is "toute en oralité, en hardes dépenaillées" (245) [wrapped in
the tattered rags of orality]. Abdelkebir Khatibi writes that his French
and Arabic mix to create "phrases en guirlande, enlacées à mort: in-
déchiffrables"[9] [garlands of phrases, intertwined to the death: undeci-
pherable].[10] Elsewhere, he equates French with a foreign woman "belle
et maléfique étrangère" [beautiful and malevolent foreign woman; my
translation].[11] Students who are in the process of learning a second language see their own difficulties and moments of joy and pleasure mir-
rored or, rather, articulated in texts that either celebrate the "infinite
hospitality of language"[12] or mourn the historical obstacles that not
only dislocated the native language[13] but also led to a mutilated and in-
complete definition of the mother tongue.[14]

   Such courses do not have to radically change the way in which our
profession envisages "French" studies: their presence in a catalogue
would not force universities to dismantle departments, to create new
ones, or to change job descriptions. But they would not reinforce our
current structures either, which is a way of saying that I cannot think
in terms of reform vs. revolution. What such courses do, if anyone no-
tices, is to expose the relative arbitrariness of our disciplinary foundations. In a sense, we all know that already. In practice, if the revelation

8. Assia Djebar, *L'amour, la fantasia* (Paris: Albin Michel, 1995).

9. Abdelkebir Khatibi, *Amour bilingue* (Paris: Fata Morgana, 1983), 11.

10. Khatibi, *Love in Two Languages*, trans. Richard Howard (Minneapolis: University of Minnesota Press, 1990), 4.

11. Abdelkebir Khatibi, *La mémoire tatouée* (Paris: UEG, 1971), 13.

12. Hélène Cixous, "My Algeriance, in Other Words: To Depart Not To Arrive from
Algeria," *Stigmata: Escaping Texts*, trans. Eric Prenowitz (New York and London: Routledge, 1998).

13. Patrick Chamoiseau, *Chemin-d'école* (Paris: Gallimard, 1994).

14. Jacques Derrida, *Monolingualism of the Other or The Prosthesis of Origin*, trans.
Patrick Mensah (Stanford: Stanford University Press, 1998).

leads to the creation of a research unit or the hiring of one faculty member, it is potentially earth shattering. But an interest in the international variations of the "French" language does not have to be confined within the limits of departments of French: such projects could also be accommodated by departments of linguistics. Similarly "literature in French" could be part of a department of "literatures" (that would also study texts in English and in Spanish for example). And the study of France or Quebec (the nations) could be seen as the typical object of study of multidisciplinary research centers that include history, economy, politics, and literature. What we know as departments of French has traditionally meant not the study of "French," but "the study of literature written in French in France" and any change might produce some institutional and individual sense of confusion, gain, and loss.

On the other hand, confusion, loss (a sense of marginalization, for example), and gain (a sense of new empowerment) have always existed in traditional structures. Typically, Francophone studies have been the province of pioneers or of dissidents, and pioneers or dissidents can be proud or humble, conquerors or oppressed opponents. I think that the best among them are capable of two forms of humility. Pioneers know that they are starting from scratch and are at risk of mimicking a centralized canon whose new authority they are already beginning to suspect, while traditionalists are still happily ignoring it, or scoffing at it. Dissidents know that they occupy the margins of a system that they need in order to operate. In certain states, schools, and departments, Francophone studies are in a position to represent what Spivak calls the "vague, menaced, and growing body of the teachers of culture and literature who question the canon" and who are "not *oppositional* any more" because "[W]e seem to be perceived as the emerging dominant."[15] Or, as some of my colleagues will hasten to point out, and as I remind myself after a depressing meeting or an irritating memo, it could be that even a marginal sense of power is an illusion: sometimes, I don't know how to decide who has the illusion of power and who clings to the illusion of disempowerment.

THE LAND OF THE UNHOMELY

"In the house of fiction you can hear, today, the deep stirring of the unhomely. You must permit me this awkward word—'unhomely'—

15. Gayatri Spivak, "Teaching for the Times," in Anne McClintock, Aamir Mufti, Ella Shohat, eds. *Dangerous Liaisons: Gender, Nation, and Postcolonial Perspectives* (Minneapolis: University of Minnesota Press, 1997), 470.

because it captures something of the estranging sense of the relocation of the home and the world in an unhallowed place. To be unhomed is not to be homeless, nor can the unhomely be easily accommodated in that familiar division of the social life into private and public spheres."[16]

The idea that "Francophone studies" have a "home" is an analogy, a starting point. Like images of parasites and definitions of the professional and of the amateur,[17] references to "homes" can easily be naturalized but they can also be used as theoretical models to make us think differently as long as we are aware that their rhetorical power is not inherently liberating or progressive. Bhabha writes:

Where the transmission of "national" traditions was once the major theme of a world literature, perhaps we can now suggest that transnational histories of migrants, the colonized, or political refugees—these border and frontier conditions—may be the terrains of world literature. [449]

As cautiously as he does, I am suggesting that "Francophone studies," as a discipline, can be imagined as a type of unhomeliness, a form of consciousness or hermeneutic sensitivity that we first recognized as the defining features of our privileged objects of study (migrant texts, migrant authors of hybrid literature, postcolonial intellectuals).

What, then, am I ultimately willing to defend when I think about what it means, in 2003, to be identified as a student of "Francophone" literary and cultural studies? The first historical by-product of my commitment to Francophone studies is a lack of faith in "Knowledge" in general: after all, Universal Knowledge (a.k.a the transparent canon) is one of the concepts successfully dismantled (for me) by a whole generation of postmodernist thinkers. Either the death of "grand narratives" has contributed to the emergence of Francophone studies or it represents one of the symptomatic changes that led to the re-evaluation of literature as a discipline. I welcomed the opportunity to take a second look at the effects that nations, markets, and universities produce when they help a whole community acquire literary references because it forced me to think about how groups share knowledge and take credit for their common literary folklore: to what extent, and among which groups, do literary references form a social cement? Due to the popularity of "récitations" in French elementary school, many grown-ups I know will remember whole passages from Le Cid (Mon bras, qui tant de

16. Homi Bhabha, "The World and The Home," in Dangerous Liaisons, 445–55.
17. See Marjorie Garber, Academic Instincts (Princeton University Press, 2001).

fois a sauvé cet empire ... ,[18] [My arm which has so often saved the realm ...]),[19] or from Victor Hugo's *La légende des siècles* (Vêtu de probité candide et de lin blanc ... [20] [robed in white linen and in probity ...])[21] or Charles Baudelaire's *Les fleurs du mal* (Homme libre, toujours tu chériras la mer ... [Man creature free, forever will you keep / The sea dear to our breast ...]).[22] Was the fact that references were shared more significant than or at least as significant as the references themselves? In other words, is any literary canon capable of producing national cultural effects, the type of comfort or passionate feelings of belonging that a flag can elicit? If I can talk about Monsieur Jourdain's naïve discovery of the omnipresence of prose, is it because I was made to memorize whole scenes from the *Bourgeois gentilhomme* or because the allusion *qua* allusion was repeatedly used in conversations around me? If Marcel Proust's "Madeleine" appears in rap singer's lyrics, has the national canon changed, or have canonical effects not changed at all? Has French literature been watered-down, reduced to a cheap commodity[23] or was it always a commodity that only upper-middle classes pass like the butter around posh dinner tables?[24] What makes me so sure that Francophone studies, that our critical tools, are not already commodified?[25]

I don't know that "Francophone studies" *must* be studied by everyone, but I do know that the issue of how Maryse Condé's Guadeloupean or diasporic novels fit in with Claire de Duras's *Ourika* or Chateaubriand's *Atala* in a literature course, or on the shelves of the same book shop, will allow me to ask different questions.

* * * * *

18. Pierre Corneille, *Le Cid,* Act 1, scene 4, line 241 (Paris: Bordas, 1984).

19. Pierre Corneille, *The Cid,* trans. John Cairncross (London: Penguin Books, 1975) Act 1, scene 4, 1.241.

20. Victor Hugo, "Booz endormi" (*La légende des siècles*) in *Victor Hugo, the Distance, the Shadows: Selected Poems,* trans. Harry Gust (London: Anvil Press Poetry, 1981), 207.

21. Victor Hugo, "Boaz Asleep" (*La légende des siècles*) in *Victor Hugo, The Distance, the Shadows: Selected Poems,* 117.

22. Charles Baudelaire, "L'homme et la mer/Man and the Sea" in *Selected Poems from Les fleurs du mal. A Bilingual Edition,* trans. Norman Shapiro (Chicago: The University of Chicago Press, 1998), 24–25.

23. See Alain Finkielkraut, *The Defeat of the Mind,* trans. Judith Friedlander (New York: Columbia University Press, 1995).

24. See Pierre Bourdieu, *Distinction: A Social Critique of the Judgment of Taste,* trans. Richard Nice (Cambridge, Mass: Harvard University Press, 1984).

25. See Emily Apter. "CNN Creole: Trademark Literacy and Global Language Travel," *Sites* 5.1 (Spring 2001): 25–46.

As long as I remember that there was a time when one had to justify one's interest in Caribbean literature (Is Césaire "marketable"?), I will not feel like asking anyone to justify his or her interest in France's literature. I cannot replace one canon with another. On the other hand, if a scholar of French studies chooses to ignore everything that is or was written outside of the Hexagon, then he or she should probably rename him or herself a specialist of Hexagonal literature rather than of French literature (though I don't think that we are about to witness the emergence of many "Hexagonal" programs of study). More importantly, I need different sets of ethics depending on which definition of Francophone studies (which context of knowledge transmission) we are talking about: distinct understandings of "Francophone studies" can and perhaps should co-exist when the members of a department are discussing course rotations, and when we are talking about the status of the profession (are we trying to help a graduate student find a job, or are we thinking about our own job, about publishers, about grants, about moving to another university?). If I ask, for example, whether "French studies" include "Francophone studies" or whether "Francophone studies" include "French studies," a different answer obtains when I am writing an entry for an encyclopedia, or when I am discussing interviewing techniques with a student who has applied for a position in a department of, say, "French and Italian" in the United States. Theoretically, Hexagonal literature is a branch of Francophone studies. I would hasten to qualify my statement if anyone mentioned reception, publishers, and spheres of influence, but I would not change my mind radically. On the other hand, if I were helping a student write a c.v., that is, prepare a sort of tactical intellectual self-portrait, I would probably advise against the idea that, as part of a course on Francophone authors, s/he might perhaps include Lamartine just to make sure that the Hexagon is not completely ignored. Not that I would suspect (most of) my colleagues to be put off by the provocative reversal—just the opposite, I would be afraid that it is too much of a neat symmetry to be theoretically interesting.

I am not interested in allowing any nation to *rayonner* or shine through its language (even if that language is my native tongue) or to police the use of languages, and I am not eager to be seen as someone whose ultimate goal is to boost enrollment in French departments. In other words, I recognize my absence of neutrality in my desire to move away from two definitions of *Francophonie*: one that would imagine a hegemonic status of French linked to a colonial power as if by some sort of perverse umbilical cord, and a second definition that would suspect non-European Francophone writers of alienation if they choose to write in French. To borrow René Depestre's lovely image, I envisage French as one of many threads used on a multicultural "métier à métisser" (the multiweaving loom).[26] I also reject the notion that the validity of our intellectual endeavor (the study of Senegalese literature in French, for example) is caught in a vicious spiral, i.e. studies in French need to be attractive to US students to make sure that professors of studies in French survive in the US. In other places, what we do when we teach "Francophone studies" here in the States may appear under different banners, different institutional umbrellas. But I do put my hopes in all the intellectual enterprises that draw attention to the precondition of our critical debates: the comparison between different nationally institutionalized definitions of "Francophone studies,"[27] and the scrutiny of the intersection or zones of estrangement between Francophone, postcolonial, or cultural studies.[28] I suspect that the hermeneutic energy that we mobilize when we try to recognize, formulate, name, and select different forms of legitimization of this academic field reveals much about our values.

I would hope that such transnational and transdisciplinary encounters between types of Francophone studies would lead to a sort of "unhoming" of the field: it would make us perceive our discipline not as "homeless" (Francophone studies do have a space in the institutional home) nor exiled (home is not somewhere else), but as struggling with unhomeliness, where legitimacy is a ghost that we keep conjuring up.

---

26. René Depestre, *Le métier à métisser* (Paris: Stock, 1998).

27. For recent studies published in France, see Jean-Marc Moura, *Littératures francophones et théorie postcoloniale* (Paris: PUF, 1999): Serge Gruzinski, *La pensée métisse* (Paris: Fayard, 1999); Michel Wieviorka, *La différence* (Paris: Balland, 2001), and Michel Wieviorka and Jocelyne Ohana, *La différence culturelle* (Paris: Balland, 2001).

28. For studies published in the United Kingdom, see Siân Reynolds and William Kidd, *Contemporary French Studies* (London: Arnold, 2000), and Jill Forbes and Michael Kelly, eds., *French Cultural Studies* (Oxford: Oxford University Press, 1995). In the United States, see Marie-Pierre Le Hir and Dana Strand, *French Cultural Studies: Criticism at the Crossroads* (Albany: SUNY Press, 2000).

SANDY PETREY

Language Charged with Meaning

Working on the reasonable principle that "periodic reviews of institutional arrangements are useful,"[1] the Modern Language Association recently compared members' participation in its scholarly and pedagogic
divisions—literary criticism, twentieth-century American literature,
women's studies, and so forth—for the years 1984 and 2001. For those
of us committed to French and Francophone studies, the changes across
those seventeen years are fascinating. In 1984, the MLA's twenty most
popular divisions included one French topic, twentieth-century French
literature. No French topics make the top twenty for 2001. In 1984, no
Hispanic topics were on the list. In 2001, twentieth-century Latin
American literature was.

Given general professional trends over the last two decades, it's not
surprising to find that the contemporary non-English literature of most
interest to the MLA's membership as a whole is now Latin American
rather than French. The decline of French and rise of Spanish are also
apparent in the MLA's lists of the ten most popular divisions devoted
solely to foreign-language topics, on which twentieth-century French
literature and twentieth-century Latin American literature have
switched positions. French, number one in 1984, is number two in
2001. Latin American, number two in 1984, is number one in 2001.

The most interesting feature of the foreign-language divisions in
2001, what the *MLA Newsletter* calls the "one significant change" (4)
in a list that has remained impressively stable since 1984, however,
isn't how French compares to Spanish. It's which components of French
studies make the list. In 2001, medieval French dropped off and Fran-

1. Phyllis Franklin, "Organizing the MLA Convention," *MLA Newsletter*, Fall
2001, 4.

YFS 103, *French and Francophone*, ed. Farid Laroussi and Christopher L. Miller,

133

cophone literature and culture came on for the first time. To pursue the
pop-music analogies invoked by top-ten calculations, Francophone
study made its debut marked with a bullet. It entered the list in sev-
enth place. Medieval French was tenth out of ten in 1984.

Although diagnosticians have often seen French studies as weak
and growing weaker, therefore, at least one component of the field has
robust vital signs bright with promise. Francophone inquiry is on the
rise, in terms of student as well as faculty interest, and it would be asi-
nine for those devoted to other components of our profession not to
welcome it with enthusiastic support. The broad array included under
the Francophone rubric has infused new life into student interest and
new paradigms into scholarly profiles. Its progress has been invigorat-
ing for the field as a whole.

The arguments for supporting Francophone inquiry are of course intellectual and moral as well as pragmatic. It's no longer permissible for
serious academics to act as though metropolitan culture alone counted,
as though only literature written in and for a European context re-
warded attentive study. Francophone orientations have done good
things for the ways French professors think and write as well as for the
number of students in their classrooms. It should enrich French departments of the twenty-first century as it has inspirited them at the
end of the twentieth.

Yet the Francophone turn presents danger as well as promise for
French studies as a whole, the danger of so dispersing the activities of
French departments that they lose their definition as coherent enterprises. To move away from the metropolis has the positive *political* effect of undermining the idea that a center is necessarily more important than anything on the periphery. But it can also have the nefarious
disciplinary effect of introducing so many peripheries that the center
cannot hold. And if the center disappears, metropolitan biases won't be
the only thing to fall apart. Departments and curricula will vanish as
well. In order for Francophone and French studies to prosper together,
they must form a dynamic whole.

Compare the avenues opened by Francophone studies to those created by the area it replaced among the MLA's most popular foreign-
language divisions, medieval French. Students of the French Middle
Ages can and do specialize in any number of fields: scholastic philosophy, oral traditions, interactions among Latin, French, and the other
Romance languages, peasant revolts, the staging of mystery plays, and
on and on. Regardless of special interests, however, the primary cur-

ricular and pedagogic function of French departments' medievalists has been to integrate their work into the rest of the department, to interact meaningfully with study of the other areas that constitute French studies. Work on peasant revolts or the staging of mystery plays might well lead to interdisciplinary study through and with other departments. But the principal purpose of this interdisciplinary study is to vitalize the discipline that constitutes the reason for being of every French department: studying French culture, literature, and language.

University study of Francophone topics opens areas more diverse than medieval studies. Yet the same principle remains imperative when Francophone inquiry takes place within a French department. A university's administrative and curricular divisions exist only so long as their identity and purpose compel recognition. Whatever dissipates their identity, whatever undermines their purpose, signals not new life but impending death. Insofar as the Francophone turn enriches, broadens, and problematizes the study of French, it is a boon to French departments. Insofar as it invalidates, dismisses, or repudiates the study of French—insofar as Francophone inquiry becomes Francophobic inquiry—it is noxious to French departments and to the faculty, including the Francophone faculty, within them.

Francophone inquiry has two definitions, one encompassing all areas outside France where French is spoken, the other addressing only those French-speaking areas that were once French colonies in Africa and the lands of the African diaspora. In the broader sense of Francophone inquiry, the Francophobic problem has never to my knowledge arisen. Has any member of a French department yet claimed that the best way to study Maurice Maeterlinck is in relation not to French poetry but to Belgian culture as manifest in Flemish communities? The normative approach to Jean-Jacques Rousseau situates him within the French Enlightenment, not in relation to experiences described in German and Italian by those who, like Rousseau, were born in Geneva. The canon of authors traditionally grouped under the rubric "French literature" includes many figures with powerful intellectual and emotional connections to cultural spaces other than France. Within the French department, however, those connections are always secondary to the linguistic and cultural space that gives French departments their reason for being.

The postcolonial cohort of Francophone inquiry, however, has raised vigorous objections to the primacy of France and French within French departments. The argument is that salient connections lead not from Francophone to metropolitan culture but from Francophone culture to the languages and experiences of the former colony in which it developed. Insofar as that experience privileges not French but Arabic, Caribbean Creoles, the linguistic pluralism characteristic of sub-Saharan Africa or the countries that were part of French Indochina, responsible instruction must follow suit. In order to understand what Mariama Bâ or Tahar Ben Jelloun writes, the logic runs, we must orient ourselves not toward those who have also written in the language they chose, French, but to those with intimate links to the world they described. Since this world has little in common with France, France has little to contribute to our understanding of what Bâ, Ben Jelloun, or other Francophone authors write.

In an article she entitled "A New (Mé) Tissage: Weaving Black Francophone Literature into the Curriculum," Margaret Moore Willens vigorously states the idea that teachers need to direct students away from France in order to present Francophone literature properly. Willens strongly disagrees with those who would relate Francophone texts to European counterparts and takes as an example of what *not* to do by setting Oyono's *Une vie de boy* beside Stendhal's *Le rouge et le noir*. Such parallels between Francophone and French literature arrogantly impose alien criteria on works that must be approached through non-European, noncanonical perspectives. "An understanding of French literature of the Caribbean and sub-Saharan Africa must go beyond a reading that seeks replication of canonical texts and themes," argues Willen. *Authentic* understanding of that literature must "seek indicators that valorize these different cultures and provide a counterpoint to Eurocentric values."[2] From this perspective, by no means unique to Willens, the purpose of introducing Francophone texts into the French classroom is not integration but separation, not harmony but "counterpoint," not comparison but dissemination.

No matter how great its ideological benefits, such a perspective will have doleful effects on university French departments. If our classrooms fully respect the fact that every cultural artifact is specific to the culture from which it came, we obviously must not relate Senegalese novels, say, to Haitian novels, or poetry from Cameroon to poetry from Martinique, or everyday life in Indochina to everyday life in Mauritius. The various entities of the Francophone world are at least as distinct

---

2. Margaret Moore Willens, "A New (Mé) Tissage: Weaving Black Francophone Literature into the Curriculum." *The French Review*, April 1996, p. 762.

from each other as from France. As a consequence, seeking "indicators that valorize these different cultures" means respecting each culture's distance from the rest of the Francophone world no less than its distance from Europe. The curriculum in search of those indicators will inevitably be an endless series of snapshots with zero chance of becoming an album. Every cultural artifact presented will insistently require demonstrating uniqueness rather than relationships. Classes must change focus as well as topic whenever they move from one part of the Francophone world to another, for the unifying force formerly provided by the "Franco-" in Francophone will no longer be available.

Resistance to employing France as a focus, to comparing Francophone literature to its French counterparts, has become a constant theme of arguments for directing classroom attention to the Francophone world. In an essay insisting that the "réalité spécifique à l'Afrique"[3] is indeed specific to Africa, for example, Angèle Kingué and Odile Cazenave argue for teaching African women's literature without any reference to women's literature from anywhere else. To avert the harm Eurocentric analogies can cause, they contend, students must be shown that "madness in the African novel has nothing to do with Western female hysteria, but rather it most often expresses the character's inability to cope with her sufferings" (646). For Kingué and Cazenave, therefore, using Emma Bovary to illustrate female protagonists' inability to bear up to suffering brings darkness rather than light, as for Willens using Julien Sorel to illustrate male protagonists' alienation precludes sensitivity to oppression. In the opinion of these and other proponents of curricular transformation in the French department, change will be meaningful if and only if the new curriculum cuts itself off from what was there before.

In contrast, I believe that every gap between French curricula that exclude Francophone culture and those that include it will have noxious consequences for the French department and for those who find their professional identity within it. The goal should be not to emphasize the (undoubted) differences between African women's and French women's despair but to show how each can illuminate the other, how representation of each shares with the other not only the French language but complementary visions of existence as a woman in societies that do not value women's existence. Although I confess to harboring

---

3. Angèle Kingué and Odile Cazenave, "Pour l'enseignement des écrivains femmes africaines dans le cours de français," *The French Review*, April 1997. p. 644.

the humanist perspectives that make such a comparative approach intellectually appealing, my argument here is pragmatic rather than philosophical. Curricula, like the departments that offer them, exist to establish links, not to eliminate them. Francophone and French culture can survive together only if each has something to say, something interesting and useful to say, about the other. To insist that one is unconnected to the other is to imply that a department offering the two has no intellectual, academic, or administrative justification. No such department deserves to survive.

Many of the most eloquent defenders of Francophone culture share my humanist perspective and haven't the slightest hesitation in asserting that study of the Francophone world and study of the French world are and must be connected for the simple reason that both are part of the human world. In their hugely influential "praise of Creoleness," for instance, Jean Bernabé, Patrick Chamoiseau, and Raphaël Confiant emphasize that serious concern with Creole practices requires us *"to show what, in those practices, bears witness to both Creoleness and the human condition"* (emphasis in original).[4] In other words, Francophone and French experiences, Creoleness and humanity, are always an amalgam, never independent entities. It is incumbent on us as teachers of French and Francophone cultures constantly and insistently to emphasize this connection, to oppose the voices urging the opposite, the voices loudly proclaiming that the periphery is necessarily dismissed if we relate it to what once appeared to be the center. We can bring Francophone culture into French departments either by emphasizing differences or by opening dialogues. Foregrounding the dialogic is in my opinion the only way to incorporate Francophone culture while also respecting French culture and the academic units concerned with it.

In one form, arguments against relating Francophone culture to France have gone so far as to suggest that the French language is itself to be repudiated. French is the language the colonists imposed on the colonized. Its every phoneme oozes Eurocentric delusions. The task of the Francophone instructor is not to introduce students to Arabic or Caribbean Creole so they may better appreciate works written in French but (again, separation instead of integration) so they may better appreciate the extent to which Francophone culture stands apart from

---

4. Jean Bernabé, Patrick Chamoiseau, Raphaël Confiant, "In Praise of Creoleness." *Callaloo* 13 (1990), 898.

French. For decades, for centuries, the sound of French served as civilizing-mission camouflage for racist oppression of the most brutal sort. Even if the oppression ended with the colonists' return to the metropolis, the language remains infected by the colonists' actions. French is a language charged with meaning for those who live outside France as well as those who live within it. But the meanings with which the language is charged are contradictory. As a result, teaching the culture of former colonies means that we must not structure a curriculum around French but must instead examine how a sensibility structured itself in opposition to it. From this particular Francophone perspective, the definition of French as the target language has undergone a radical shift. French is now a target because it deserves to have weapons hurled at it rather than because a faculty and a curriculum take it as the target of their pedagogic efforts.

Any number of celebrated pronouncements by Francophone writers who have felt oppressed by French could serve as examples. The one I want to quote now first appeared in the *New York Times* as I was writing this essay. The *Times* ran a long story about the Algerian novelist Mohamed Moulessehoul, who recently revealed that he is the (male) author of the novels published under the pseudonym of the (female) author Yasmina Khadra. The story, like Moulessehoul's adventure as a whole, raises fascinating problems about the nature of identity, about the relation of the former colony to the metropolis, about the intersections of gender and race, and about other topics crucial to contemporary studies in postcolonialism.

But the story contains a quotation typical of a large, a very large number of Francophone novelists. Moulessehoul has written his books in French, yet he defines his relation to that language as distant and alienated. His views are striking. "I have trouble speaking French well. French is my writing language, my language of introspection, solitude, isolation, reflection, concentration, but never my language of daily communication. For some Arabs, to speak French is to perpetuate colonialism."[5] How should we, members of French departments, react to statements like that? Should we encourage our students to concentrate on the subaltern status French imposes on those who use it although it is not their native language? Or should we rather encourage students to ponder the fact that, no matter how great the alienation, a huge number of authors from the Francophone world have chosen French as the

5. *New York Times*, 21 February 2002, E5.

language in which they write their books, through which they communicate what they have to say, by which they establish their artistic identity? As far as I'm concerned, those of us who teach French can give only one answer to such questions. The integrative thrust crucial to every curricular organization requires us to privilege the "writing language" over the spoken language, for it is the writing language that brings the works of Moulessehoul and other Francophone authors into the French classroom.

Nevertheless, for certain commentators, the French classroom should concentrate on validating the extra-French aspects of Francophone cultures, the aspects that move away from the French language and French culture. The argument is that only by leaving France and Europe behind can we liberate students from Eurocentric ideologies and the horrors for which they have been responsible.

No matter what our reaction to such ideologies, however, it's essential to recognize that repudiating Eurocentrism also repudiates any academic departments that have French and France as their justification. In other words, the energy implicit in the fact that Francophone inquiry is on the rise while other components of the French curriculum are on the decline can eviscerate as well as invigorate French departments. If the new energy is directed away from French and against France, departments whose justification is teaching French and learning about France will be victims rather than beneficiaries.

It's important to be clear here. My concern is not the relative merits of studying France versus studying Cameroon, Cambodia, Guadeloupe, or any other part of the Francophone world *in the abstract*. It's the effect of eliminating France's traditional role *in a French department*. Even for those who categorically and unreservedly refuse to privilege Europe in any way, the problem of how to approach non-European topics must appear different in a department devoted to a European culture and one with a more open orientation. It's not by accident that French departments, French curricula, and French professors all have "French" in their names. They exist because of French. To disown French is to threaten their existence.

Disowning French has been explicit as well as implicit in arguments for augmenting a department's Francophone component. Margaret Moore Willens, for instance, appears to prefer texts written in Creole to those written in French. As she sees it, "writing in a language which is not the writer's first language is problematic enough, but add to that the knowledge that the second language is a means of oppression and paradox can lead to anguish or even tragedy." In preference to French and what has been written in it, Willens chooses Creole and what has been spoken in it, favoring those who speak "in defense and illustration of the spoken language as well as in revolt against the language of oppression" (767).

Once more, those of us committed to university instruction in French must consider such positions pedagogically as well as politically. I find it egregiously unproductive to tell my students that I expect them to write and speak a language that is not their own and that, to inspire them to do so, I will devote a great deal of class time to showing why writing and speaking that language is oppressive, stultifying, and racist.

Think about this for a while. What kind of students are we likely to find in French classrooms if we present French as the "language of oppression" and devote ourselves to showing how foul the oppression was? Who would want to study a language defined by the person teaching it as racist, vulgar, and offensive to every right-thinking person? The only candidates I can think of are neo-Nazi skinheads, white-supremacist survivalists, and other misfits who want to master the language of oppression because they get a huge kick out of practicing the techniques of oppression. Since these are (presumably) not the sorts of students we want in the French classroom, I find it impossible to understand why colleagues consider it fruitful to define the French language as a means of oppression.

Of course French can be oppressive, stultifying, and racist. But it can also be liberating, exhilarating, and glorious, as it has been for a huge majority of those who figure in the Francophone canon. Mohamed Moulessehoul, whose strictures against French I just quoted, nevertheless chose French as the language in which he wrote his novels, made his reputation, played his games around identity and gender, created the persona that makes the *New York Times* quote him. The same could be said of any number of Francophone authors, all of whom are by definition *Francophone* authors no matter how ambivalent their feelings about French. It's true that French has been a language of oppression, a means of oppression. So has every other language in human history. But French (like many other languages in human history) has also been a language of exuberant self-realization, of declarations of rights, of fulfillment and actualization of inspiring human potentialities. In other words, French, like every other language, has served both admirable and nefarious purposes. To emphasize the nefarious over the admirable while trying to interest students in studying French is suicidal stupidity.

French's role as a language of liberation is by no means limited to the performative power it has exercised in Europe. It has been a medium of freedom for a striking number of authors outside Europe as well. For those of us in French classrooms and French departments, for those of us devoted to making Anglophone students understand *why* we are in French classrooms and French departments, it's far shrewder to emphasize what has made the French language a liberating force than what has made it a colonial horror.

It's also shrewder to emphasize the *French* language over the various dialects more or less connected to it that have developed in the Francophone world. However advisable it might be for those who already know French well to appreciate the fact that standard Parisian isn't the only form of communication in French, introducing the multiplicity of alternate forms to classes with minimal ability to distinguish one from the other is certain to make even more difficult a task that's already difficult enough: learning a foreign language.

For some defenders of the Francophone turn, however, only sustained presentation of a multiplicity of linguistic forms can rescue students from the idea that some versions of French are better than others. In a recent article in the *French Review,* Sharon L. Shelly approvingly quotes those who argue for acquainting students with sociolinguistic variables "even at the elementary level" in college and "in beginning secondary school courses as well."[6] Shelly sees metropolitan French as valuing clarity and perfection whereas Caribbean speech raises different standards "in opposition to these ideals." As she puts it "Francophone Caribbean literature offers linguistic irregularity, orality, and a conscious deformation of the French language" (115). The Francophone turn demands that we teach our students deformation rather than formation because "we cannot promote Francophone cultures while ignoring or denigrating the variable forms of the language code in which these cultures express themselves" (115).

Shelly goes further. We must not only introduce variable forms of French, we must make it clear to our students that these are not substandard languages but validly autonomous means of communication in their own right. "Creole is a rule-governed language in its own right,

6. Sharon L. Shelly, "Addressing Linguistic and Cultural Diversity with Patrick Chamoiseau's *Chemin-d-'école." The French Review,* October 2001, 113.

not simply a 'defective' form of French" (117). This perspective requires that Creole, like any other language used in the Francophone world, be presented not through its connections with French but through its separateness from French.

And again the Francophone-French axis becomes the Francophone-French abyss. What I have been arguing for in this paper, integration of French and Francophone studies, becomes impossible if defenders of Francophone culture believe it can be taught only on its own terms, not in relation to the language and culture that led to its designation as Francophone. I haven't the slightest doubt that every aspect of Francophone culture can indeed be productively and instructively taught on its own terms. But every aspect of that culture can also be taught through the links between it and the rest of the Francophone world, including metropolitan France. In the French classroom, the only sensible way to teach it is to foreground connection over renunciation, infusion over repudiation. When E. M. Forster first used the phrase, "only connect" was a moral imperative. For teachers of French in the American academy, it is a matter of life and death as well.

At a time of diminishing resources, the problem of how best to modernize instruction is intimately bound up with recruiting and hiring those who will be responsible for it. The dynamism and growth of Francophone studies make it a premier field for recruitment by French faculties. Yet it's essential to remember that this recruitment has as its purpose vitalizing rather than abandoning French studies. Our teaching and research must have a core in order to have a shape and a purpose. The only candidate for that core is French and France. It's incumbent on recruitment committees to recognize that Francophone interests alone are not enough, that those interests can be harmful if they cut themselves off from the center of every French department in every institution of higher learning in the United States.

Consider the result if a French department actually did renounce the centrality of France and French to provide egalitarian instruction on all areas of the Francophone universe. Valuable though it is for a French department to incorporate (for instance) Quebec, Mali, Guadeloupe, and Morocco into its academic purview, that purview will disappear unless France and French—the factors that put Quebec, Mali, Guadeloupe, and Morocco together in the first place—retain their organizational and instructional primacy. No department of any kind can adequately teach the huge variety of Francophone cultures. The only plausible candidate for selecting and organizing the aspects of those cultures to be covered in a French department is France. This is not because of some essential quality making France different but because of the historical realities that allow us to apply the term "Francophone" outside of Europe. Why does a French department teach the culture of Senegal rather than that of Zimbabwe, the literature of Martinique rather than that of Jamaica, the history of Indochina rather than that of China? Solely because Senegal, Martinique, and Indochina have connections with France and French that Zimbabwe, Jamaica, and China do not. A French department that attempts to teach students about the Francophone world without emphasizing the factors that linked that world to France is doomed to collapse intellectually as well as administratively.

In the twentieth century, French literature was enriched by several authors from non-Francophone countries. Samuel Beckett was Irish, Eugène Ionesco Rumanian. More recently, the Czech Milan Kundera has taken French as the language of his novels, and the Nobel laureate Gao Xingjian works in French as well as Chinese. All the writings of these figures lead away from France, in one case just about as far away from France as it's possible to get without leaving the planet. But they also lead to France, to the culture and language that constitute the matrix of their creativity. Integrating them into the curriculum of a French department unquestionably opens students to worlds beyond France, but it also highlights and spotlights the value of the worlds inside France.

I take the contribution of figures like Beckett and Kundera to the French curriculum as a model for the place of Francophone figures within it—prominent but integrated and organic. It would make no sense to teach Joseph Zobel's *La Rue Cases-nègres*, for example, without highlighting its validation of the culture that animates the non-French environment named in its title. It would make no more sense to teach it without concentrating on what French culture means within it, nothing less than the means by which it came to be written and the form in which it is read. Zobel's protagonist-narrator appropriates French as well as endures it, and it is this appropriation that offers the best opportunity for connecting this and similar novels to the rest of the French curriculum.

Another model bright with promise for Francophone studies is the relationship between Latin American and peninsular cultures in Spanish departments. It was twentieth-century Latin American, not Spanish, literature, that replaced twentieth-century French literature as the only foreign-language topic among the MLA's most popular divisions, and the Western hemisphere has been more responsible than Europe for the spectacular recent gains of Spanish in the American academy. Those gains have produced exactly the enrichment of the Spanish curriculum Francophone studies can bring to the French curriculum, but the gains were possible only because professors of peninsular and Latin American literature agree—unreservedly and enthusiastically agree—that the language that matters to them is Spanish. This is the primary language for all the cultures studied in Spanish departments, and French departments will need a comparable focus to attain comparable levels of productive integration.

Besides harmony on the sense of "target" in "target language," different sections of Spanish departments share appreciation for one another's cultural achievement to an extent not always found in relations between French and Francophone specialists. Jorge Luis Borges wrote "Pierre Menard, Author of *Don Quixote*," not "Pierre Menard, Author of *Tierra del Fuego Tales*" or "Pierre Menard, Seer of Andean Authenticity." Borges obviously did not consider his Argentine identity polluted or defiled by connecting his work (all his work, not just the Pierre Menard fantasy) to European literature, an attitude matched by contemporary Spain's respect for the achievements of Hispanic cultures on the other side of the Atlantic. The works most responsible for Latin American literature's current prestige are not only written in the Spanish language but also have a thoroughly symbiotic relationship with the mother culture, a thoroughly symbiotic relationship that French and Francophone studies need to emulate.

Spain's relation to Latin America is of course not at all the same as France's to its former colonies. In the context of university study, however, the fact that students of Spanish culture in and outside Europe collaborate synergistically can and should inspire French and Francophone students to do the same. Francophone culture has a vital place in French departments of the twenty-first century only so long as specialists of that culture understand why they are in a French department.

LAWRENCE D. KRITZMAN

A Certain Idea of French: Cultural Studies, Literature and Theory

> It is a sign of contraction of the mind when it is content, or of weariness. A spirited mind never stops within itself; it is always aspiring and going beyond its strength; it has impulses beyond its power of achievement. If it does not press forward and stand at bay and clash, it is only half alive.
>
> —Montaigne, "Of Experience"

Once upon a time, in the not so distant past, the French department was the "in" place to be. It was the *locus* of intellectual ferment and the center of avant-garde critical thought in the American university. Most everyone in other humanities programs and the humanistic social sciences suffered from French theory anxiety. French thought, often an object of ridicule in the New World, now became an object of intellectual fetishism. From the 1960s on, French criticism became associated with "theory" and its practitioners were engaged in naming an enemy that was most often incarnated in a humanistic tradition that valued the methods of History and the Subject. What some reductively characterized as "*la pensée 68*" found its adversaries in those who proclaimed the importance of the work of reason and human consciousness.[1] Those boutique French theorists, Derrida, Foucault, Althusser, and Lyotard, declared the end of metaphysics in the name of a newfound radicalism that abandoned universal values in favor of language games and discursive networks. In the so-called age of the "death of the author," this group of theorists, ironically became *maîtres à penser*, and gave French studies a certain cachet. In short, we had entered the

1. See Luc Ferry and Alain Renaut, *La pensée 68* (Paris: Gallimard, 1985).

YFS 103, *French and Francophone,* ed. Farid Laroussi and Christopher L. Miller, © 2003 by Yale University.

glamorous age of designer theory and with it came a fascination for things French.

Today, however, we find ourselves in a somewhat different historical context. Within the American university some French departments have lost their fashionability in terms of critical theory. In some cases, theory has been replaced by an insipidly narcissistic personal criticism (as distinct from true memoir writing) whereas in other instances the Anglo-American institution of literary studies has now engaged in the unchecked growth of a critical industry inspired, in part, by a simulation of 1970s French thought. At times this phenomenon has degenerated into an epidemic of sorts that has become the critical equivalent of safe sex: "condomized theory" or theory without consequences. Whatever the positive or negative aspects of the various poststructuralisms in their heyday (when they functioned as radical practices), the goal of their theoretical imperative was to explode the presuppositions of all existing institutions. But now lo and behold we have become the victims of pseudotheories that have been merchandised and sold according to the exigencies of a consumer-oriented university culture that has left us abandoned in a morass of repetitive indifference engineered as a neo-positivistic enterprise.

To make matters even worse, French studies has witnessed the departure of certain of our colleagues who have totally defected from the discipline of French to departments of English, comparative literature, and Anglophone cultural studies in recent years. This was done, so they claim, because of the Eurocentrism and elitist attitudes of French programs (and some of this was indeed true) and the perception that fighting the good fight was now being played out in the politically hip universe of English speaking literatures. In short, doing things French (and this was often viewed in terms of the specificity of the Hexagon itself), was no longer considered cool; it was a luxury item and therefore easily disposable. Indeed many of those *émigrés* uncritically accepted English as the *lingua franca* of the day (a form of linguistic imperialism if there ever was one) and for the most part multiculturalism was seen to be everything other than the study of language itself.

If I evoke the current situation, it is in order to better situate some of the issues confronting the field today. The arrival of Francophone studies in American departments of French is a good case in point, although it is difficult to situate its originary moment. When I was an undergraduate thirty years ago, writers such as Césaire, Fanon, and Senghor were an integral part of the curriculum in the department of French at the University of Wisconsin at Madison, so I didn't quite understand the unease in some quarters when Francophone studies appeared to be labeled an "emerging" area of study. Not all colleagues welcomed this new development with suspicion. However, for those who confronted it as a challenge (particularly in terms of the competition for enrollments), it represented an incursion into the clearly delineated space of French culture.

As I have attempted to demonstrate in another context, much of the packaging of French studies in the postwar period in the United States was based on the ideology of the nation and the so-called civilizing mission of France.[2] Much of the approach to teaching "French" grew out of the inherited Republican tradition of Jules Ferry who believed that a dissemination of the humanitarian ideals of the Enlightenment tradition would enable the nation to reclaim its greatness through language, customs, and genius. Quite clearly this cannot be viewed simply negatively as an example of how the empire struck back. Yet it must be understood that the study of French was not just that of its national literature in an American setting; it was based on an *aesthetic* of civilization whose universal imperative took the form of public virtue. Many of us, as I have previously described, were subjugated to a certain idea of France and accordingly, like the French themselves, remained committed to the horizontal development of the modern-nation state. Often forgotten and sometimes even ignored were those colonial and postcolonial cultures in which French was thoroughly imbricated.

Yet the introduction of Francophone studies, a phenomenon that sometimes happened simultaneously with the development of cultural studies, had both its positive and negative effects, what I term the "either or" syndrome projected by the pedagogical fundamentalism of some of those on either side of the divide. Those who were implicitly threatened by the development of Francophone studies uncritically conflated it with cultural studies (as if cultural studies was exclusively reserved for non-Hexagonal French language communities) and reified their positions, as imaginary aristocrats, in the name of cultural Francophilia. Often in an uncritically reductive gesture they saw these new developments as a threat to the pedagogical imperative underlying French studies. Sometimes they asked us to choose naively be-

2. See Lawrence D. Kritzman, "Identity Crises: France, Culture and the Idea of the Nation," *Substance* 76/77 (1995): 5–20.

tween Descartes and French rap and by doing so created a dislocation (a barricade of sorts) between civilization and its discontents. The imaginary community of the French department that was founded through this process was legitimized through the invention of a mythic idea of *"francité,"* a phenomenon that functioned as a political authority or the equivalent of a disciplinary police.

Some of the proponents of Francophone studies have also divided the world according to the binary pattern of good versus evil. There is a danger here stemming from the desire to foreground the so-called "other" in a reductive manner (in a way we are all others and we all speak in borrowed tongues), whereby the "other" falls victim to an essentialism that is entirely one. This pedagogical imperative can lead to idealizing such constructions in the pieties of a naive multiculturalism, tending toward a dangerously unreflected oversimplification produced by the practitioners of a born-again humanism.

Ethnic humanism or identity politics implies that there is some sort of essence or foundation to humanity even in its diversity. Many of the more naive approaches to multiculturalism ironically fall victim to the same idea of the Cartesian *cogito* that underlies much of modern Western metaphysics and asserts its self-identity by eradicating anything outside of itself, that is to say alterity in its multiple manifestations. This less enlightened approach to multiculturalism in some French programs has appropriated the European definition of the human by adhering to anthropological universals that suggest an appeal to a series of generalized presuppositions concerning the nature of oppression. If, as some claim, identity is constituted by differences, the imperative to define the other as the negative of the same confirms the argument put forth by Edward Said in which ethnicity (i.e. cultural differences), as I believe he defines it, is defined as the abject object of the subject of and in power.[3]

Here Derrida's notion of monolingualism should be taken into account to interrogate the dangers of the Western philosophical notion of identity, which in some cases today has degenerated into a form of political moralism. In analyzing culture we need to understand that we cannot take hold of identity and that it must be seen as nonessential, nonfoundational, and defined by individual particularity of context.

3. Edward Said, *Orientalism: Western Representations of the Orient* (New York: Pantheon, 1978).

Because of the mediation of language we must realize that language is something that the subject cannot possess, for to claim possession of language would imply essence in identity. Identity may be given to us by language, but like identity language both mediates and is mediated by social contexts and individual vectors of identification. If as Derrida suggests, "I have only one language; it is not mine," it is because we all carry elements of the other within the self and all modalities of identification are foreign. To be sure, if identity is constantly in flux and therefore "of the other," the phantasmatic modalities of identification ironically foreground the irreducibility of alterity:

> My "own" language is for me, a language that cannot be assimilated. My language is the only one I hear myself speak and agree to speak in the language of the other.
> This abiding "alienation" . . . is neither a lack nor an alienation; it lacks nothing that precedes it or follows it, it alienates no *ipseity*, no property, and no self that has been able to represent its watchful eye.[4]

One of the difficulties with texts such as Franz Fanon's *Wretched of the Earth*, if treated as a metatext, is that it thematizes the narrative of decolonization as a universal dialectical struggle since, as he claims, "the colonial world is a world cut in two."[5] The danger of ascribing theological significance to texts such as Fanon's, in spite of their ability to make us aware of the dynamics of subordination, is that in advocating an "ethics of recognition" and the Hegelian idea of the "self coming to itself," the cost of universality, as Christopher Miller suggests, "is a bit of cultural specificity."[6]

In order to get beyond the Hegelian structure of colonizer/colonized underlying moralist pedagogy and delineated in texts like that of Fanon, it is necessary to see the terms of the equation in a relationship of cross fertilization. Unfortunately Fanon scripted the narrative of decolonization as a universalized dialectical struggle in which the colonial subject violently came into being and assumed recognition. In quite a different perspective, Homi Bhabha has focused on the dialogic exchange of colonialism as a "hybrid displacing space" of cultural

4. Jacques Derrida, *Monolingualism of the Other or the Prosethesis of Origin* [1996] trans. Patrick Mensah (Stanford: Stanford University Press, 1998), 25.
5. Franz Fanon, *The Wretched of the Earth*, trans. Constance Farrington, preface by Jean-Paul Sartre (New York: Grove Press, 1963), 29.
6. Christopher L. Miller, *Theories of Africans: Francophone Literature and Anthropology* (Chicago: University of Chicago Press, 1990), 58.

transactions that get beyond the essentialist paradigms of pedagogical idealism and the infelicitous consequences of self-containment.[7] To be sure, in this context Derrida's critical examination of Levinas's same-other relationship can enable us to transcend the totalizing violence of recognition and to conceive of the other as a convergence of traces of a nonpresent otherness. If culture cannot be identical to itself, it is because the very idea of hybridity constitutes a "third space" whose discursive energy undermines the forced cohesion of contested sites. Here, as in the work of Derrida, the cultural analysis of texts should enable us to be hospitable to alterity, for the performative act of critical reading functions tropologically like a catachresis that foregrounds the faults in the paralyzing myth of identity politics.

In American universities, the teaching of French is currently facing three different challenges: the restructuring of academic interest around interdisciplinary research and programs; the need for a broader understanding of French as France has entered into a more global world in recent years; and the imperative to reaffirm the importance of French language study itself as a means of foregrounding the cultural and historical specificity of our pedagogical imperative. Whereas the prestige of French thought remains strong (simply witness the plethora of translations into English), many of the theoretical and intellectual tools that were developed by French thinkers have now been absorbed by other disciplines, are taught in translation, and are used to study other cultures. One of the many challenges before us is to successfully integrate the study of culture in a meaningful way within French departments so as to enable our students to obtain interdisciplinary training and to engage in the study of language in its many textual manifestations.

Teaching in French is critical not only for the understanding of the diversity of French language cultures, but it may also be the linchpin for the survival of the discipline itself. If, as some have already done, we eliminate the use of French in the teaching of French culture we will eliminate that which is at the very core of what we do. If, for instance, literature can be taught without allowing for language difference, we would then reject the idea that thought and language intersect, and instead transform thought into an idealization that is produced independently of language.

As I have explained in another context, our students need to gain cultural competence, the ability to comprehend cultural patterns in

7. Homi K. Bhabha, *The Location of Culture* (New York: Routledge, 1994), 226–27.

terms of their multiple meanings, their syntax, and their interrelationships within a global context. In our attempt to engage in cultural hermeneutics concerning the identity of French, it is imperative to get beyond the overdetermined ideology of what French should be and transcend pedagogically what Gerard Noiriel has described as "the French construction of the sense of belonging."[8] What is at stake here is the transposition of the ideology of the nation into the classroom.

Yet how utterly naive some of us have been when we believed that a theoretical revolution had taken place that was to have altered our pedagogical practices. Theory, at least for me, was supposed to explode institutional presuppositions and challenge the consequences of accepting unchallenged hierarchies. But, alas, sometimes the opposite has happened. In fact some of the "imaginary aristocrats," the counterrevolutionary forces of today (who don't understand the ethic of *noblesse oblige*) have reified their positions in the name of "a certain idea of France." In "French Studies/Cultural Studies: Reciprocal Invigoration or Mutual Destruction," the critic of nineteenth-century French literature Sandy Petrey, in a somewhat strident tone, demonstrates a certain ambiguity concerning the relationship between the study of culture and intellectual endeavor.[9] He invents a hegemonic power struggle, a caricature of sorts, a conflict where a perilous enemy is declared: French cultural studies, which he defines, at times, in a monolithic way. In his analysis, Petrey conceives of it as a threat to "the historic mission of French studies" and suggests that this critical *praxis*, a mere ploy to augment enrollments, might very well bring about its demise.

In a way Petrey articulates a hegemonic construction of a French language community whereby unity, like Renan's idea of the nation, is subject to strategies of exclusion, totalization ("The French classroom needs not to dissolve identity but to solidify it," he proclaims [390]), and forgetting. He makes reference to expressions such as "a certain idea of France" (391), "the canonical French authors," and finally defines the discipline as one that is a "field based on canonical arts and cultural francophilia" (386) and being "part of the high culture of European civilization" (385). While he claims that he is "politically sympathetic" (391), he declares: "the desire to read figures like Voltaire in

8. See Gérard Noiriel, *Tyrannie du national* (Paris: Calmann Lévy, 1991).
9. Sandy Petrey, "French Studies/Cultural Studies: Reciprocal Investigation or Mutual Destruction," *French Review* 68 (1995): 381–92.

the original was a determinant factor in creating the success of French courses in the past, and if we discard those figures we need badly to replace them with an equally strong motivation for studying with us. King Daddy Yod is not it" (391). Who, may I ask, is asking us to abandon Voltaire? In fact a better grasp of the paradoxically constructed Voltairian notions of tolerance and democracy might help us understand the symptomology of contemporary social phenomena as they are represented in the many discursive forms of popular culture. Petrey asks us to choose between Voltaire and King Daddy Yod and by doing this he has essentially created a dislocation (a barricade of sorts) between French and its so-called others. This institutionalization of presuppositions, and the insertion of this nostalgic, albeit melancholic view of French, establishes a series of constraints whereby the idea of "*le bon sens*" is represented in universal terms, but which, however, cannot but be contestable. The "imaginary community" that he wishes to reaffirm is one that is legitimized through the invention of a mythic origin construed as a political authority.

Petrey calls cultural studies "a floating signifier" (384) while at the same time straight-jacketing it within the Anglo-Saxon model (i.e. Richard Hoggart and Stuart Hall and the Birmingham School) whose empirical shape is invested in the belief that hegemony is derived from the imposition of cultural priority. Such an ontologically loaded approach to the study of culture forecloses on its hybridity and engages in an essentialism of those on the margins. Indeed the very danger of constructing a cultural view in this manner is that it disables the alterity of the other from exceeding itself and renders the empirically based *praxis* of the study of culture unethical in its paralytic appropriation of otherness.

The study of French should be conceived rather broadly to cover a wide variety of hermeneutic practices that delineate how a multiplicity of singularities are produced within multicultural French language communities and the varieties of expression (for example, Creole) and the indigenous linguistic systems that have functioned within them (for example, in North Africa, Arabic and Berber). As I see it, cultural analysis concerns itself with symbolic and discursive representations that must be studied as an intersection of relations of difference in historical context. If, as I have suggested previously, we must not simply reinforce the ideology of universalism in the classroom, what then does the term "French" signify in the expression "French Studies"? We have not yet found a meaningful way to delineate how the modalities of the

Hexagon and and the many "Francophone" literatures partake of the world, and how this may affect the curriculum. Often non-Hexagonal literatures play the role theory did some twenty-five years ago: they function like the chocolate truffle at the conclusion of a meal, a paradoxically conceived luxury item or perhaps even worse, a side-dish.

If we are to engage in "French studies" we must enlarge the field of observation to include all areas where Francophone languages are spoken, even though some of those languages are tainted with the imprint of a colonial past. This activity requires, at least for the modern period although not exclusively, a multicultural form of interdisciplinary work that includes textual and linguistic practices studied in a transcultural manner, in short, hermeneutic strategies that are both comparative and dialogic in nature. This approach would require, as Joan Scott has suggested, more than a simple attempt to compose counter-histories of the oppressed. It would require an epistemological analysis of how "subject positions" are negotiated in the process of writing and how so-called "othered subjectivity" is ironically grafted onto the culturally proper:

> Making visible the experience of a different group exposes the existence
> of repressive mechanisms, but not their inner workings or logics; we
> know that difference exists, but we don't understand it as constituted
> relationally. For that we need to attend to the historical processes that,
> through discourse, position subjects and produce their experiences.[10]

Like Barthes's atopic site of seduction in *A Lover's Discourse*, the negotiations between self and other must be seen as referring to the relation itself. In so doing, they ironically demonstrate that if "the truth of the master is in the slave," it is the result of the impropriety of this *pas de deux*.[11] With this in mind, indeed we as pedagogues cannot refer to "la France" as a kind of Heideggerian *Stimmung*, but instead must conceive of it as a phenomenon whose latency engenders and acknowledges a debt to the other.

In opting for a space for the study of culture within a French program, by no means am I suggesting that we eliminate from the curriculum our century-oriented study of literature according to periodization. However, as of late, the more reactionary among us have

10. Joan Scott, "Experience," in *Feminists Theorize the Political*, ed. Judith Butler and Joan Scott (New York: Routledge, 1992), 25.
11. Jacques Derrida, *Writing and Difference*, trans. Alan Bass (Chicago: University of Chicago Press, 1978), 255.

assigned literature a more specified institutional status by limiting it to aesthetic considerations and defining it as that which it is not (i.e. history, politics, philosophy). To be sure, as Adorno has suggested, the nature of the so-called aesthetic experience is in itself an ironic phenomenon since the sociocultural is both separate from and implicated in it. "Art," claims Adorno, "is autonomous and it is not; without what is heterogeneous to it, its autonomy eludes it."[12] The cultural study of literature demonstrates how discursive formations problematize what they represent and how aesthetic and sociocultural considerations intersect and contest one another as a means of transcending epistemological boundaries and as a way of foregrounding critical latencies.

In studying texts and other cultural objects we must transcend the divisionality of literature (as perhaps some of the great writers in the French language tradition have done: Montaigne, Descartes, Malraux, Césaire). Literature cannot be regarded as something distinct and closed nor should cultural studies, as some practice it, entail everything other than the study of literature itself. It should be seen as part of the phenomenon of culture and become a heuristic device for the articulation of discursive, epistemological, and social relationships. To be sure, we are still living according to the exigencies of the model put forth by the nineteenth-century German university. For example, we should not forget—as some of us have—that science and literature once functioned in a dialogic relationship that allowed for epistemic transfers between scientific knowledge and the literary project. Far from being separate areas of human thought as exemplified in American universities with their colleges of Arts and Science and in the French division between "Faculté des Lettres" and "Faculté des Sciences," science and literature are in fact imbricated in one another and are fully developed by their cross-fertilization.

The most institutionalized form of literature, too, the so-called great texts, must be rediscovered and through them we must adopt what Michel Pierssens has termed an "epistemological attitude" that will enable us to foreground the critical role of literature in the production of knowledge and as "possible model for other disciplines in their conceptual formations."[13] We need to make a concerted effort to diversify our curriculum and to study texts and culture within a

12. Theodor W. Adorno, *Aesthetic Theory*, trans. Robert Hullot-Kentor. (Minneapolis: University of Minnesota Press, 1997), 6.
13. Michel Pierssens, "Literary Studies and the End of History," *Substance* (1996): 6–19.

broader framework. We must return to a nonfundamentalist approach to theory by using the texts of the target language (French) as a means of discovering how knowledge is born through a variety of symbolic representations. *La théorie est morte, mais vive la théorie.*

In some cases, the interminable ennui produced by the senseless attacks on the canon has sometimes trivialized the intellectual issues at stake. There can be no doubt that we have all benefited intellectually from the inclusion of texts written by women and minorities and that we must resist the Allen Blooms among us who wish to push us back to the future. Nevertheless, the cultural study of texts demands a reclaiming of an inheritance that we can make "pervertible" through the violation of the codification of cognitive rules. Those who criticize the reading of the canon see it as what Pierre Bourdieu once described as a practice of reproduction and consecration. While it is true that the institution of literary studies can be legitimized in that way and thereby attain "cultural capital," it would be unwise solely to view all inherited literary culture, as Bourdieu suggests, as a "field of restricted production."[14]

To be sure, rereading the canon is an intellectual necessity, and it should operate neither as an uncritical act of inheritance nor as a neutralizing process of knowledge that contains diversity. The passive appropriation of tradition can only foster a universalizable epistemological model capable of undercutting the destablizing dimension of critical thinking. In contrast to this, what Michel de Certeau characterized as "oppositional practices" is a way to confront the hegemonic power inscribed in canonical texts through operations of diversion:

> I call a tactic a calculated action determined by the absence of a proper locus. . . . A tactic has no place but that of the other. Thus it must play on and with a terrain imposed on it and organized by the law of a foreign power.[15]

The culture that lives by "the information of the book" is, according to de Certeau, predicated on the rule of an elite whose very authority is derived from the power of the *logos.* Tactical thinking is therefore construed as an act of resistance to standardized reading or a "rhetorics of

14. Pierre Bourdieu, *The Field of Cultural Production,* trans. Randall Johnson (New York: Columbia University Press, 1993).

15. Michel de Certeau, *The Practice of Everyday Life,* trans. Steven Rendall (Berkeley and London: University of California Press, 1984), 36.

reading," which Michel Charles describes as a way in which texts carry within themselves the constraints that legislate readerly modes.[16]

De Certeau's notion of tactical reading can be useful in its attempt to come to terms with institutionalized knowledge through a symbolic challenge. Yet, however laudatory de Certeau's destablizing gesture of putting into question the homogeneity of the canon may seem, it appears to be more temporally focused on transcending the constraints of the past. In this context the historian Roger Chartier cautions us to be attentive to the social conditions in which the act of reading is produced and accordingly suggests that the readerly act of appropriation "in the present" also operates prospectively as a kind of virtual knowledge.[17]

Instead of relying on interpretative tactics as a way to liberate literature from its fetishistic relationship to the past, textual exegesis focused on the question of inheritance can allow us to reformulate the historicity of experience in relation to its futurity or the power of iteration realized as a movement to the wholly other:

> The condition of which the future remains to come is not only that it be known, but that it not be knowable as such. Its determination should no longer come under the order of knowledge. . . . It is a question of this performative to come whose archive no longer has any relation to the record of what is, to a record of presence of what will have been actually present.[18]

As so-called custodians of literature and culture we should become skeptical of academia's quest for pure knowledge and the tranquility of primal grounds. Cultural legacies constitute an opening up to the virtual, which is always already beyond the present. Inheritance should therefore be regarded as a temporal modality, activated by critical thinking, and whose very being is predicated on divergence. In terms of literary culture, inheritance implies a politics of memory, which, as Derrida suggests in *Specters of Marx*, "is never a given . . . and is always a task," a reading in response to the other's text. If archival memory (the textual matter of our pedagogical enterprise) evokes both past and

16. Michel Charles, *Rhétorique de la lecture* (Paris: Seuil, 1977).

17. Roger Chartier and Pierre Bourdieu, "La lecture. Une pratique culturelle," in *Pratiques de la lecture*, ed. Roger Chartier (Marseilles: Rivages, 1985).

18. Jacques Derrida, *Archive Fever*, trans. Eric Prenovitz (Chicago: University of Chicago Press, 1995), 72.

future, the latter can only take shape through the virtualities that be-
fall inheritance.

Reading as a pedagogical practice should begin as an act of perjury
enabling the reader to invest outside of the inherited matter inscribed
in the text and to transcend the institutional foreclosure on alterity:

> An inheritance is never gathered together, it is never one with itself. Its
> presumed unity, if there is one, can only consist in the *injunction to
> reaffirm by choosing.* One must means *one must* filter, sift, criticize,
> one must sort out several different possibilities that inhabit the same
> injunction. And inhabit in a contradictory fashion around a secret. If the
> legibility of a legacy were given, natural, transparent, univocal, if it did
> not call for and at the same time defy interpretation, we would never
> have to inherit from it. We would be affected by it as a cause—natural
> or genetic. One always inherits from a secret, which says "read me, will
> you ever be up to do so?"[19]

If, for example, one regards universalism as "a sovereignty whose
essence is always colonial," one must nevertheless engage with that
very heritage in order to demystify the presuppositions that underlie
what Robert Young has termed "white mythologies."[20] By engaging
with texts in this way, the institution of literature can be opened to
time so that the misrecognized object of the inheritance makes itself
receptive to the event of alterity.

The deconstructive tradition can therefore enable us to challenge
the tradition of French universalism and a cultural politics that adheres
to the uniformity underlying the idea of the nation. As Derrida demon-
strated nearly twenty five years ago, Lévi-Strauss's analysis of so-called
primitive thought had appropriated its difference so that it could be assimilated to the logic of Western reason. Quite clearly thinking in this
vein may allow us to "decolonize" the prejudices of Western ethno-
centrism and engage in an asymmetrical relationship to alterity.

By challenging universalism and the logic of identity upon which it
is built we shall enable our students to think of the discipline of French
otherwise. A possible model for this may be found in Jean-Luc Nancy's
notion of the "unworked community."[21] In the case of Francophone

---

19. Derrida, *Specters of Marx*, trans. Peggy Kamuf (New York, Routledge, 1994),
16.

20. Robert Young, *White Mythologies: Writing History and the West* (London: Routledge, 1990).

21. Jean-Luc Nancy, *The Inoperative Community*, trans. Peter Connor, Lisa Garbus,

studies (which paradoxically should include the Hexagon), we need to delineate its "disjunctive ratio" by drawing attention to its shared "singularity." This means that we need to avert the Benettonesque canned euphoria derived from the illusory adherence to the motto of "we are the world" and instead engage in identificatory practices that paradoxically find their strength in the unworking of the forced community.

To go beyond the knowledge of the prescriptive we need to reaffirm the importance of critical theory and regard such an endeavor as an ethicopolitical responsibility. By returning to theory we can avoid the totalizing imperative underlying most of American academia's institutional performatives and question the universalist assumptions produced in the Hexagon and still permeating some of the pedagogical translations of French culture into an American context. The reaffirmation of the importance of theory can render our readerly engagements with texts subject to precontractive agreements whereby the problematic notion of ends and transmission underlying the ontotheological nature of the teaching of the canon may be put into question. One can only hope that the promise of the future may be found in reconsidering the line from *Hamlet*, "the time is out of joint" (which Derrida has analyzed in *Specters*), as symbolic of the desire to disappropriate the contractual bonds of the inherited injunctions produced by a certain "*lagarde et michardisme*" and thereby discover pedagogical freedom in making our students countersign culture's iterability.

What is therefore at stake in reinvigorating some programs is a commitment and a desire to get beyond the stereotypical and to take intellectual risks. To accomplish this we must realize that the very notion of a certain idea of French is one that cannot be paraphrased through the mediation of the professor qua representative of the "*syndicat d'initiative.*" Indeed the performative act of teaching French can resist conformity by opening a chasm between the imaginary and the symbolic and thus enable us to ask questions and transcend the symptomatic melancholia of what French studies once was. Welcoming the other into what has traditionally been called French studies requires neither the assimilation that has been characteristic of the integrative model of nationhood nor the appropriating gesture of empowering what has been viewed by some in the past as "the subaltern." On the contrary, what is required is the call of the ethical that takes specula-

Michael Holland, and Simona Sawhney, ed. Peter Connor (Minneapolis: University of Minnesota Press, 1991).

tion beyond collective agency so that the promise of the future can no longer be found in the impropriety of making French studies proper. As readers professing the *studium litterarum* in French, our engagement with texts can only begin when we engage in critical resistance to pre-fabricated meaning and abandon the belief that knowledge can ever truly be mastered.

Postscript:
In Memory of Naomi Schor

NAOMI SCHOR

Feminism and Francophone Literature: From One Revolution to Another[1]

The title of this panel invites two approaches: on the one one hand to wax nostalgic for the good old days when Hexagonal French literature reigned in smug self-congratulatory splendor; on the other, to sing the praises of a new era when the canon has been augmented by a rich and vital corpus of Francophone literature. I wish to do neither. Rather, I would like to share the musings of a scholar who participated in the last great revolution in the redefinition of the French canon. In short, I want to speak as a feminist.

Let me begin by stating that I intend no simple amalgamation of women's and Francophone writing, nor is one either possible or desirable. Aside from the fact that both pose the ever vexed question of the criteria for inclusion of a body of work previously excluded from the tightly policed precincts of the canon, they differ in any number of ways that would need to be patiently teased out. Women's writing, as it was initially construed, was conceived of as a universal category, transhistorical and transnational, whereas Francophone writing has from the outset been viewed as a federation of distinct writing practices, embedded in a shared (but by no means universal) history of colonialism. One might speak of a Francophone archipelago. Or, to put matters another way, there is no common measure between the utopian search for a hypothetical specifically female language, which was carried on in what I now think of as high feminism—a brief moment in the early eighties—and the complex forms of diglossia at work in so-called Francophone writing. Not only are their relationships to the master's tongue not homologous, except by means of a metaphor, women's writ-

1. This title has been added by the editors. The title of the conference panel referred to in the first sentence was "Paradigms Lost and Found."

YFS 103, *French and Francophone,* ed. Farid Laroussi and Christopher L. Miller, © 2003 by Yale University.

ing and Francophone literature are not mutually exclusive categories: as black American feminists were quick to point out in the eighties, black women's writing was doubly excluded, for one form of exclusion often masks another. Finally, feminism, that is Western feminism, sometimes finds itself torn between its double allegiances. Thus, as Emily Apter notes in "French Colonial Studies and Postcolonial Theory," a propos of Hélène Cixous's *Vivre l'orange,* which was written at the time of Khomeini's rise to power: "As a French *pied noir* and a Jewish feminist, Cixous found that despite her self-identification as an exiled, semi-Third World subject, she had difficulty being open minded about religious difference when that difference entailed an orthodoxy drastically restrictive of human rights (as defined by Occidental norms)."[2] There is finally the brute fact that whereas so called Franco-feminists sought to constitute a counter-canon that would complement the Canon, there is within the Francophone community a separatist strain that wishes to establish a canon of its own, which would stand apart from, rather than enhance, the metropolitan canon.

One could go on, but I wish to come to what I see as the crucial question, and it centers on the word *paradigms.* One of the claims made by feminists was that what we were calling for was not simply the inclusion of un- or underread writing by women in a canon largely constituted by the proverbial dead white males, but for a paradigm shift, what was then called "reading otherwise." As some witty feminists put it, the recipe for this new way of reading was not "add a woman and stir." What they were pointing to was the need for a new pot. To introduce a new ingredient is according to the most elementary laws of cookery to transform the basic stock. Now, it would appear, the critics of Francophone literatures are making the same claim, as though canon-enlargement is in every generation bound up with a call for a thorough transformation of the ways one reads. As I muse, I ask myself did feminism indeed produce a way of reading otherwise, and what remains of it? Will Francophone and, more generally, postcolonial studies in their turn produce new modes of interpretation, and what traces will they leave?

The over-arching question—"How has the study of literature changed with the arrival of Francophone literatures?"—requires a double answer. One: Francophone literatures did not arrive alone and did

2. Emily Apter, "French Colonial Studies and Postcolonial Theory," *Sub-stance* 24/1–2 (1995): 169–180.

not arrive first. The dismantling of the Enlightenment universal handed down, and nowhere more so than in and by France, was well underway by the time Francophone literatures emerged. Indeed their emergence may be viewed less as a cause than as an effect. And two: this question presumes the persistence of one eternal element, which is the study of literature itself. But as the lesson of Cultural Studies has reminded us, literature itself is not an unchanging given, not impervious to history. This is the challenge we all must meet.

TOM CONLEY

From Detail to Periphery: All French Literature Is Francophone

—In memory of Naomi Schor

Naomi Schor, our close friend and colleague for whom we grieve in this collection of essays that Christopher Miller and Farid Laroussi have assembled, has shown us that the beauty and force of literature are felt when it is treated in all of its detail. Her studies capture things minuscule that she makes scintillate as she arrives at conclusions of universal proportion. Focusing on Zola, Sand, Balzac, or Chateaubriand, she locates crucial points where language and image or where speech and things conflate, explode, and radiate luminous energies. Her work has been—and will continue to be—a model of reading that we can strive to follow. In her teaching, too, Naomi seized upon turns of expression where meaning suddenly becomes strange, where it opens onto new spaces, and wherever, in the very least, it invites close and extensive scrutiny.

For all of us she has been a champion of the alienating powers of literature. She has shown us that her literary heroes and heroines of nineteenth-century France were forever transfiguring their verbal matter into things seen, into *choses vues* that had often been overlooked by champions of literary positivism. Conversely, in her studies of art and artists—on the walls of her imaginary museum hung paintings by Delacroix, Géricault, and Millet, and on the floors stood the sculptures of Duane Hanson adjacent to those of Rodin—her modern masters encrusted their pigment, stone, or acrylics with verbal matter. Shards of language turned these things into *objets lus*, into forms where writing and images turned back and forth into one and the other. She continually turned words into elegant shapes that were other than what they

YFS 103, *French and Francophone*, ed. Farid Laroussi and Christopher L. Miller, © 2003 by Yale University.

were said to mean, and she transformed paintings and drawings into things riddled with language, with matter otherwise foreign, but always vital, to their material substance. In her fabulously personal work on postcards she delected in clichés that were literally underwritten by the words of family, tourists, or lovers sending greetings to their kin and friends.

In the same vein, in her close readings of literature Naomi Schor has led us to reconsider the components that comprise the "discipline" or the "canon" of French studies from new points of view. Sometimes they inhere in the works themselves ("Emma, c'est moi," says Flaubert . . .), but more often than not they stand outside of them (Flaubert infers that the author of *L'éducation sentimentale* identifies neither with Frédéric Moreau nor Madame Arnoux . . .). Her studies of conflicting viewpoints reveal, too, that identification is a function of distanciation, and that the play of proximity and distance with respect to a work of literature or art transforms it from a fetish into a productively critical object. Following the inspiration of her writing, I shall contend that Naomi Schor has taught us a salutary truth that will carry French studies far into the twenty-first century. From the multiple perspectives she employed in her studies of French writings of the post-Revolutionary era, she affirmed for us, sometimes obliquely and sometimes directly, that, if it can reach the difficult and tenuous expression required of it, *all French literature is Francophone.*

None of her favorite authors was ever really Francophone, but she succeeded in turning them into writers of that signature without needing to speak of their alterities or differences as such. With the exception of Baudelaire's *Les fleurs du mal,* in which exoticism belongs to a "Vie antérieure" in French colonies and to an unlikely "Invitation au voyage" anywhere out of a world destroyed by economies of territorial expansion, on cursory view the style and substance of Chateaubriand's *Le dernier des Abencérages,* Sand's *La mare au diable,* and Zola's *Germinal* do not invite comparison with words originating from French-speaking areas outside of nineteenth-century France. But they all affirm that their virtues reside in self-alienating powers that allow them to call themselves into question. She has shown that great writings always interrogate the positions whence many of their unstated or axiomatic propositions are made. Every discourse of real force, she argued, carries elements that run against its grain or that it itself cannot mange or contain. The new perspectives that we have gained on the French canon are due to an element—we can call it Francophone—that questions the very identity of writers with the works to which they append their names.

In order to understand what it means to say that all French literature is Francophone we can recall two concepts that figure prominently in Naomi Schor's critical writings. One, the *detail*, is the partial unit from which a sensuousness is felt in our perceptions of the alienating powers of language. The detail summons any seemingly self-adequate expression or statement given to carry meaning by virtue of its "common sense." The detail becomes pertinent when it does *not* reflect, lead toward, or confirm a "whole" or greater sum of which it is a part. The detail shifts between the problematic unity and partiality of its own being. As Schor often emphasized in her research on feminism and psychoanalysis, Freud was obsessed with the detail when he called the clinical picture of Dora an "autonomous" or self-contained "fragment" of a virtually "integral" partial analysis. The detail makes visible a force by which the origin, site, or even the genealogical roots of a work become subject to greater inquiry. In the bedrock of French studies, the *explication de texte*, the detail yields the paradoxical effect of putting readers *outside* areas to which they are attracted. Because it is of a proportion and scale different from its context, the detail invites speculation on literary geography, that is, on the space both of texts themselves, in their ink and paper, and of what they represent to a mind's eye.

Study of detail invokes, second, a parallel concept of *periphery* and of peripheralization. Our appreciation of detail alters the points from which we (as analysts) can speak about where the text (or analysand) is "coming from." By peripheralization is meant that what had figured as a center on a mental map now shifts toward another border or even a different cultural milieu. William Faulkner's Mississippi is now being seen as much from the Caribbean as it had been from the literary establishment of New York. Camus is situated as much in the Maghreb as an author affiliated with the Éditions Gallimard on the rue Sébastien-Bottin in Paris. Éluard is a traveler who follows to some degree the footsteps of Victor Ségalen, displacing himself from the New Hebrides or points of surreal travel where he longed to be or was never able to live. If a general law can be obtained from the impact of Francophone studies on the geography of the French canon, it would assert that what had been understood to be reflective of France and the constitution of the nation, especially in manuals of literary history of the last century, tends to come from forces on the edges or borders that push toward the inside from without. As a corollary, when a literary object is scrutinized in detail, its own virtues pertain to geographies of difference. Literature that does not cannot qualify to be either French or Francophone.

To see how this happens, we can recall in greater detail Naomi Schor's compelling reading of Freud's obsession with things minuscule. In "Displacement," chapter four of *Reading in Detail*, she notes that "the detail in Freud functions in opposition to the fragment."[1] Although "the two terms are occasionally used interchangeably," for Freud "the fragment is to the detail as the ancient is to the modern, as depth is to surface, as scarcity is to surplus, and as construction is to interpretation" (66). Fragments belong to a world seen through the lens of archaeology whereas the detail "is directly linked to the psychopathology of everyday life." Finally, the fragment is a "solid and detachable part-object," bearing a masculine valence, while a detail is feminine (67) because therein the psychoanalyst's "own femininity is encoded" (68). She later notes that the detail in each of Freud's casehistories "is not seen as referring metonymically back to a whole from which it had become detached" (72) in a logically cohering order of the world and its parts, "but rather as substituting metaphorically for another detail which it resembles," what she calls "a detotalized detail" (72), of no easy proportional measure in respect to other details. Excess and repetition become their pertinent traits. They also turn a textual surface into a surface of disparate pieces of incalculable meaning, of fetish-like shapes that refuse to release the meanings the viewer or reader would wish to find in them.[2]

1. Naomi Schor, *Reading in Detail* (New York and London: Methuen, 1987), 66.
2. It is instructive to follow the dialogue that the late Charles Bernheimer engages with Schor's reading of *Salammbô* (originally in her *Breaking the Chains: Women, Theory, and French Realist Fiction* [New York: Columbia University Press, 1985]) in his *Decadent Subjects: The Idea of Decadence in Art, Literature, Philosophy, and the Culture of the 'Fin de Siècle' in Europe*, ed. T. Jefferson Kline and Naomi Schor (Baltimore: The Johns Hopkins University Press, 2002). Discerning a psychoanalytic model of subjectivity in her reading, he argues that the last sentence of the novel is indeed a "'sentence-thing,'" a textual fragment that fails to "release a world of meaning," thus bringing the reader back to "the brute materiality of the verbal signifiers" (54). Everywhere, he concludes, the text is scattered with "particulars, be they body parts, bits of motivation, fragments of causal explanation, pieces of romantic rhetoric, lists of exotic practices. . . . " Consonant with Schor, he underlines the points that the perspective that would have located and valorized these objects disappears from view. The disappearance of a scale or standard of meaning would be similar to the effect of the island as a standard unit of land mass. Its relation to itself and to its own surface-effects sheds light on a bond that ties literature to cartography, especially the tradition of the *isolario*, a genre, as Édouard Glissant and others have implied, that would bear pertinent Francophone traits.

Seen in terms of a geography of peripheralization, the fragment would be a land mass detached from the continent to which it had been joined, such perhaps as the northeastern coastline of Brazil visualized as an area separated from the rectangular edge defined by the southern and eastern shores of central Africa. The detail would be one island of an archipelago-world for which no easy explanation, evolution, or pattern of expansion is available. No causality can be deduced, nor even can the form and content of one detail be seen in an adequate relation with another (one detail is not as it seems to be, nor is it quite defined by its contiguity with another). As a result, the impact of Francophone studies on the ordering and arrangement of the canon of French literature can be attributed to this kind of lacunary geography of detail. A work taken as a singularity or an accretion of details loses the centrality it would own in spaces defined by preordained literary histories. An island, it is located by its peripheries in relation to other peripheries and other islands or insularities. It would resemble the lentil-like Caribbean that Édouard Glissant has celebrated in his *Discours antillais,* or even recall the figure that the early modern cartographer Guillaume Testu, when he spelled the *Antilles* of the Columbian archipelago as *Lentilles,* likened to a literal scatter of lentils (on a map in his *Cosmographie universelle* of 1551). The detail and island would be imagined both as sites and as lenses through which different spaces and perspectives could be grasped.

French texts studied in this way would belong to a Francophone literary geography. Units of writing that spatialize themselves independently of any causal linkage with others would call for modes of investigation that synthesize the Freudian drive for detail and an implicit geography that attends to islands, to borders, to littoral and limitrophe regions. It follows that French literature becomes Francophone when its details invite speculation on centers and peripheries and on places where spatial consciousness inheres in the fungible character of printed discourse. Texts of the kind that belong to Glissant's Antilles are exemplary, but so too are works that we can read inside of the French canon from places outside of France. A litmus test of the detail and of points where French literatures becomes Francophone, a canonical moment in the history of French literature that has seduced many into the study of early modern French writing is the thirty-third chapter of *Pantagruel.*

Alcofribas Nasier, the chronicler and narrator of the deeds of his giant prince, climbs into the mouth of his maecenas. Pantagruel and his band are at war with the Almyrodes, the last faction of an enemy that refuses to surrender to the good cause of the gentle heroes. Rain falls during the campaign. Fleeing from a cloudburst while the troops gather under the cloak of Pantagruel, Alcofribas takes refuge. Hiding "dessoubz une feuille de Bardane, qui n'estoit moins large que l'arche du pont de Monstrible"[3] [beneath a leaf of a burr, that was no less wide than the arch on the Monstrible bridge], he insists that the truth of his account cannot be called in question. The *Bardane* from which he emerges is in itself a mass of details that puts scale and proportion, the measure of standards of veracity, into doubt. All of a sudden new peripheries of things are seen encrusted in the contours of the substantive. The word, of origin around Lyons, the region of origin of the first edition of *Pantagruel*, refers in local idiolect to lice and reaches back to *baruum* or "mud" in popular Latin. The *bardane* was known to stink and to grow amid detritus and rubble.[4] Here the burr is seen from several perspectives, at once as a louse and as a prickly growth that stinks and sticks to the clothing of those, including the unwitting narrator, who grazes it in passing. The *bardane* resembles a self-fortified sphere or a medieval weapon of a size and measure equal to the "Monstrible" bridge seen adjacently in the same sentence.

Alcofribas emerges from the clump of leaves, climbs up, and ambles for about two leagues on the top of Pantagruel's tongue. He follows a path beaten in similar fictions by characters in the stories of Lucian and Folengo. The narrator walks as if he were approaching the Hagia Sophia in Constantinople. He soon discovers on the horizon "de grands rochiers, comme les montz de Dannoys" (331) [huge rocks, like the Danish mountains].[5] Alcofribas then begins to wander on a surface that is both a map and a landscape, at once a cartographic image, a text, and a topographic view: "je croy que c'estoient ses dentz, et de grands prez, de grandes forestz, de fortes et grosses villes non moins grandes que Lyon ou Poitiers" (31) [I believe they were his teeth, and great fields,

---

3. François Rabelais, *Pantagruel*, in Mireille Huchon, ed., *Oeuvres complètes* (Paris: Gallimard/Pléiade, 1994), 530. Subsequent references to Rabelais will be cited between parentheses in the text above. Translations are mine.

4. In his *Dictionarie of the French and English Tongues* (611) Randle Cotgrave defines *bardane* as "[t]he Clote, burre-docke, or great burre; also, the noisome, and stinking vermine, called, a Punie." He contrasts a *bardane la grande* ("clote burre, great burre") to a *petite bardane* ("the louse-burre, ditch-burre, less burre docke").

5. Mireille Huchon notes that *Dannoys* is an "obscure allusion," a pun on *dents*, *Dannoys* uttered "dan-noué." A geographer would see a fabulous synaesthesia of the flatlands of Denmark with Alpine peaks imagined as gigantic molars and incisors.

great forests, strong and squat cities no less great than Lyons or Poitiers]. The narrator meets "un bon homme qui plantoit des choulx" (331) [a good man who was planting cabbages]. The contrast of detail is striking to the course and analogue in Lucian of the old man who grows vegetables in order to subsist. The planter in *Pantagruel* is a merchant who harvests and sells his cabbage "au marché en la cité qui est icy derriere" [at the market in the city over yonder].

The scene is marked by an unlikely profusion of contextual detail and a sense of the peripheralization of French territories in respect to a world, in the early 1530s, that is felt to be "globalizing" or changing its perspectives on itself. In Erich Auerbach's unparalleled study of the chapter in *Mimesis*, the passage is chosen to show that Rabelais coverts the strangeness of the discovery of the new world on the heels of the Columbian voyages into that of the familiar lands of regional France, most likely the Touraine or the fields around Lyons, the town whose name is printed on the title-page of the book itself. The world is thrown topsy-turvy. "Rabelais," notes Auerbach (who was said to have written *Mimesis* while in exile in Istanbul during the Second World War), "gives himself the opportunity of exchanging roles—that is, of making the cabbage-planting peasant appear as a native European who receives the stranger from the other world with European naïveté; above all, he gives himself the possibility of developing a realistic scene of everyday life."[6] Alcofribas becomes an other—and an *author*—by suddenly assuming the pose of the stranger from a new world, all the while the stranger becomes the concentrated patriot from the old world. Alcofribas swears, "Jesus . . . il y a icy un nouveau monde" (331) [Jesus . . . here there is a new world], affirming that he is in new lands that are beguilingly familiar.[7] Readers of the celebrated passage have argued that the beginnings of anthropology are found in the encounter,[8] just as, too,

6. Erich Auerbach, *Mimesis: The Representation of Reality in Western Literature*, trans. by Williard G. Trask (New York: Doubleday, 1953), 237.

7. The stranger Alcofribas suggests in his exclamation, "*Jesus . . . il y a icy un nouveau monde*," that he already knows of the new world before he arrived in the mouth of the hero, *Jesus* equivocating on the first-person preterit tense of *savoir*: "*je sus* [qu'] il y a icy un nouveau monde."

8. Terence Cave, in *Pré-Histoires. Textes troublés au seuil de la modernité* (Geneva: Droz, 1999), writes of moments that perturb the subject, such as the meeting with the cabbage planter or Montaigne's fall from his horse (recounted in II, vi of the *Essais*). With them Cave seeks to establish a topography of possible perceptions at given historical junctures. "This topography ought to allow one to define better the multiple and highly problematic border between conscious perceptions, habitual perceptions (hence partially conscious) and virtual, suppressed perceptions, or else those that can be assigned to the

there might reside in the image of *choulx* an analogy not only with little worlds for reason of the globe-like shape of cabbage, the presence of a deictic marker in the substantive that asks *where* it might be (*où* in ch*ou*lx), and the latent equivalence of rows of cabbage to those of papillas on the tongue, such that the savor of the vegetable would be found in the very field on which the sprouting plants could be imagined.

Whatever perspectives may emerge from our ongoing encounter with Rabelais's cabbage planter, when the words conveying the episode are read in detail, as both transcriptions of sounds and as visual marks of a grammar bearing a singular visibility—in the very least because its presentation has similar effects in both gothic and roman letters—the idea of a French kingdom is *peripheralized*. Dotted with place-names of the order of Lyons, the origin of *Pantagruel*, and Poitiers, a city known in a famous rebus to be an agglomeration of three round peas (*pois-tiers*), each site in itself becomes a world detached from other worlds at large. Centers and circumferences, axes and peripheries, limitrophe and familiar regions are jostled in both the perspective of the verbal representation and the graphic register of the chapter. Each word can be seen in isolation, as a detail, but also as sign of a geography of mixed proportions contained in the printed characters and flowing in the spaces between them.

The dispersive effect of the episode can now, we realize, be attributed to its own "Francophone" latency. As in new canons of French expression devoted to the study of the margins of French civilization and its formerly colonized lands, renewal and alteration come as aftereffects of encounter with and passage through different cultures. Alcofribas's meeting with the *planteur de choux* seems, in the rich psychoanalytical sense of the term, to be *introjecting* the ambivalence and insecurities that come with the fathoming of unknown regions of the world. The chapter puts them in a buccal cavity that is not yet ready to utter or name alterity as such, and as a result the meeting becomes affiliated with a long and familiar body of encounters that extend from the *Chanson de Roland* and Chrétien de Troyes to Kateb Yacine and Simone Schwarz-Bart. The force of the episode in *Pantagruel* would be attenuated if it were treated merely as a "topos," that is, as a thematic matrix that would keep the details from continually scattering, isolating themselves, and making their meanings equivocal.

---

realm of the unspoken" (18). He is, in other words, bringing a Francophone point of view to his discipline.

Naomi Schor's insistence that the detail be taken as synonymous with surface, surplus, and interpretation can be deployed to open the text onto even different peripheries and, too, be extended through a greater critical mass of literature, geography, and Francophone traditions. Auerbach and other readers of the chapter rarely study this locus classicus in French literature in the context of the *incipit* of the chapter in which it appears. The beginning, the moment when the world is invented with the first words, which break a silence as if they were the beginning of *Genesis,* is revealing. Close to victory over the enemy Almyrodes, Pantagruel and his troops advance. Alcofribas begins his summary thus:

> Ainsi que Pantagruel avecques toute sa bande entrerent es terres des Dipsodes, tout le monde en estoit joyeux, et incontinent se rendirent à luy, et de leur franc vouloir luy apporterent les clefz de toutes les villes où il alloit, exceptez les Almyrodes qui voulurent tenir contre luy, et feirent response à ses heraulx, qu'ilz ne se renderoyent: sinon à bons enseignes. [330]

> As Pantagruel with his army entered the lands of the Dipsodes everyone was joyous, and suddenly they surrendered to him, and of their free will brought him the keys of all the cities where he was going, except the Almyrodes who wanted to keep him at bay, and in response to his heralds said they would not surrender unless it was in good token.

In its detail the description at once anticipates and sums up the perspectival and peripheralizing effects of the narrator's encounter with the local farmer that will take place only a few sentences *infra.* The words generate greater quanta of detail, such that the surfaces of the signifiers give way to yet other surfaces and elicit other modes of apprehension. Through an extraordinary geographical latency felt in the movement between the visual and aural character of the words, excess is heaped upon excess. If we recall some of Henri-Jean Martin's and Walter Ong's writings about the interchangeability and locomotion of printed letters in the early modern age, for whom the historical proximity of the invention of moveable type causes the letter to sparkle on the surface of the page and to gain independence with respect to the grammar, syntax suddenly becomes paramount.[9] Words are defined in part by the

9. Henri-Jean Martin, *La naissance du livre moderne. Mise en page et mise en texte du livre français (XIVe–XVIIe siècles)* (Paris: Éditions due Cercle de la Librairie, 1998), especially 192–94 and *infra;* Walter J. Ong, S.J., "Space, System, and Intellect in Renaissance Symbolism," *Bibliothèque d'humanisme et Renaissance* 18 (1956) 226–39. See also Henri Zerner, *L'art de la Renaissance en France. L'invention du classicisme* (Paris: Flammarion, 1996), 14–16.

four cardinal directions that are implied when they are read "right side up," or when each of their letters is imagined set in a four-sided surround that holds its form and serves as a physical base in the printer's mold. Thus the words resemble and often invite comparison and exchange with the quadrants of letters in adjacent words in the same lines or in those furrowed in the text above and below. The characters that belong to given agglomerations of letters can be shuffled and rearranged, like the moveable type that conveys them, in different configurations.

Words thus become insular and modular forms subject to creative rearrangement. When subjected to the pressure of detailed reading the same assemblages of letters can give rise to unforeseen (and often surreal) analogies. The reader is not required to take printed words as they are given but to invent new and other spaces by virtue of heeding differences inhering in their aural and visual form. Something of a preliterate or infantile fancy, if not a pleasure taken in the encounter of letters and words, inhabits the very process of reading. In this sense Pantagruel's entry into the lands of the Dipsodes becomes a study of alterity of proportion and difference that has topical bearing on Pantagruel's mouth. When the prince and his *bande* entered the lands of the Dipsodes, they were virtually there prior to their arrival. When they *entrerent*, the preterit verb signaling their entry at once sums up, anticipates, and reflects the object of the quest. The men *entrerent es **terres***. As a result *tout le monde*, the entire world, reacted with joy. When the people "suddenly" (*incontinent*) surrender to Pantagruel, an array of geographical differences, all common to contemporary books of cosmographies, is brought forward. A great land mass, a continent, seems to be an extension and an analogy of the hero's body all the while it is the site of groups of urban agglomerations, *toutes les villes où il alloit*. Earth, world, land, continent, and city: all are gigantic entities, surpassing the limits of what the eye can see, that radiate from the particles of the narration. The peripheries of the world are reached within the confines of the verbal matter of the sentences describing the movement of the Pantagruelian campaign. The encounter and cultivation, indeed the welcoming of differences are celebrated where battle would otherwise merely be a typical order of things.

Detailed treatment of the graphic and thematic texture of the beginning of the chapter shows that the work is inaugurating encounter and, no less, the introjection of cultures and of people who are variously other. When studied through the lens of the detail and of its peripheries,

Pantagruel, a work often taken to be canonical and belonging to a national heritage, becomes Francophone. The meeting with the cabbage planter has as one of its grounding virtues a model of the encounter and exchange of alterities. The same virtue becomes a criterion by which "official" French literature can be included under the rubric of Francophone studies. Works such as those of Rabelais, which had figured in the patrimony of the French nation, acquire a different aspect when they are studied in the light of the literary migrations and "reterritorializations" taking place in our time.

When Christopher Miller and Farid Laroussi asked the contributors to this volume to speculate on the ways the new and emergent literatures "of French expression" from outside of the confines of France have changed the ways of teachers and scholars trained within the tradition of the canon, they were inviting us to think of things familiar from different perspectives and in the context of new geographies. There intervened the terrible death of Naomi Schor. We have since discovered that she had been responding to Miller's and Laroussi's question before it was posed and, now, that our collective sense of a rejuvenation of French studies owing to Francophone studies finds firm conceptual grounding in Naomi Schor's writing. In homage to her and to her groundbreaking work on detail we see better how and where the fabulous alterities of canonical writings come forward and call into question our habitual ways of reading and deciphering the world. We lament Naomi's passing, but we also take inspiration from her love of French literature, a literature that, for many reasons thanks to her, is virtually and totally Francophone.

Contributors

RÉDA BENSMAÏA is University Professor of French Studies at Brown University. He is the author of *The Barthes Effect: The Essay as a Reflective Text* (1987), *The Year of Passages* (1995), *Alger ou la maladie de la mémoire* (1997), and the editor of *Gilles Deleuze*, (1988 and 1998). His most recent book, entitled *Experimental Nations: The Invention of the Maghreb*, forthcoming from Princeton University Press (Spring 2003), analyzes the way different North African Francophone writers dealt with national identity, language, and cultural constructions after the independence of their countries.

MICHAEL CALL is a graduate student in French at Yale University.

TOM CONLEY, who teaches at Harvard, has recently translated and edited Marc Augé, *Un ethnologue dans le métro*, and *In the Subway* (2002). His *L'inconscient graphique: Essai sur la lettre à la Renaissance* appeared in 2000 (Presses de l'Université de Paris-VIII). He is currently working on a section of *The History of Cartography* (University of Chicago Press), edited by David Woodward, on early modern literature and mapping.

J. MICHAEL DASH is Professor of French at New York University. He has translated Édouard Glissant's *The Ripening* (1985) and *Caribbean Discourse* (1989) and, most recently, Gisèle Pineau's *Drifting of Spirits* (1999). His critical publications include *Literature and Ideology in Haiti* (1981), *Haiti and the United States* (1988), and *Édouard Glissant* (1995). His most recent books are *The Other America: Caribbean Literature in a New World Context* (1998), *Libète: A Haiti Anthology* (1999) with Charles Arthur, and *Culture and Customs of Haiti* (2001).

YFS 103, *French and Francophone,* ed. Farid Laroussi and Christopher L. Miller, © 2003 by Yale University.

DANIEL DELAS is Professor of Language Studies at the University of Cergy-Pontoise, where he teaches sociolinguistics and poetics, particularly in the field of Francophone literatures. He has written on African and Caribbean authors, and he serves as a managing editor of *Études Littéraires Africaines,* and as director of an academic series for Hachette Publishers.

SAMBA GADJIGO is Professor of French and Francophone Studies at Mount Holyoke College and author of *École blanche Afrique noire,* (L'Harmattan, 1990). He was the guest editor of *The Novels of Aminata Sow Fall, Contributions in Black Studies* (University of Massachusetts Press, 1992) and co-editor of *Ousmane Sembene, Dialogues with Critics and Writers* (University of Massachusetts Press, 1993). He is currently writing a biography of Ousmane Sembene, to be entitled *La vie d'un artiste militant.*

KAREN GOULD is Dean of McMicken College of Arts and Sciences and professor of French and Francophone literature at the University of Cincinnati. She is the author or co-editor of five books, including *Writing in the Feminine: Feminism and Experimental Writing in Quebec* (Southern Illinois University Press, 1990) and *Postcolonial Subjects: Francophone Women Writers* (University of Minnesota Press, 1996), and numerous articles and essays dealing with contemporary Quebec writing and culture, and the French *nouveau roman.*

JEAN JONASSAINT, who is currently teaching Francophone literatures in the Romance Studies Department at Duke University, serves on the editorial board of the journals *Études francophones* and *Nepantla: Views from South.* He is the author of *La déchirure du (corps)texte et autres brèches* (1984), *Le pouvoir des mots, les maux du pouvoir. Des romanciers haïtiens de l'exil* (1986), and *Des romans de tradition haïtienne. Sur un récit tragique* (2002).

AMADOU KONÉ taught for many years in Côte d'Ivoire before moving to the United States, where he taught first at Tulane University. He is now Professor of Literature and African Studies at Georgetown University. As a novelist, playwright, and scholar, Amadou Koné has published numerous books, including *Des textes traditionnels au roman modern, Étude sur les avatars de la tradition orale dans le roman ouest-africain, Les coupeurs de têtes* (a novel), *Le respect des morts* (a play). His most recent novel is *L'œuf du Monde* (Hatier, 2002).

LAWRENCE D. KRITZMAN is John and Pat Rosenwald Research Professor and Professor of French and Comparative Literature at Dartmouth. He has written extensively on early modern and twentieth-century French literature, contemporary European thought, psychoanalysis, and critical theory. His most recent works are *The Fantastic Imagination: The Mind's Eye in Montaigne's Essays,* and the editorship of the *Columbia History of Twentieth-Century French Thought.* He is currently completing a study on politics and French intellectuals.

FARID LAROUSSI is Assistant Professor of French at Yale University, where he teaches twentieth-century French literature and Maghrebi Francophone literature. He has published on literature and cultural representations (Beckett, Proust, Valery, Roussel) and on issues pertaining to identity and identification (Algerian literature, Beur novels). He is currently working on the dynamics between the French literary imagination and Maghreb culture.

CHRISTOPHER L. MILLER is Frederick Clifford Ford Professor of African American Studies and French at Yale. He is the author of three books on French and Francophone literatures. His current research is on the French Atlantic triangle and the literature and culture of the slave trade.

SANDY PETREY, Professor of French and Comparative Literature at the State University of New York at Stony Brook, is the author of *Speech Acts and Literary Theory, Realism and Revolution,* and *History in the Text.*

J. RYAN POYNTER is a graduate student in French and African-American Studies at Yale University. He is currently working on his doctoral thesis on eroticism in Francophone Caribbean poetry and fiction.

CHRISTOPHER RIVERS is Associate Professor of French at Mount Holyoke college. He is the author of *Face Value: Physiognomical Thought and the Legible Body in Marivaux, Lavater, Balzac, Gautier, and Zola* (University of Wisconsin Press, 1994), as well as numerous articles on French literature. He is the translator/editor of Adolphe Belot's *Mademoiselle Giraud, ma femme* (1870), published in 2002 by the Modern Language Association, in their Texts and Translations series. He is currently working on the French boxer Georges Carpentier (1894–1975).

MIREILLE ROSELLO teaches at Northwestern University. Her main research and teaching interests are postcolonial (Caribbean and North African) literatures and theories. She has written on Surrealism (*L'humour noir selon André Breton*), on Tournier (*L'in-différence chez Michel Tournier*), on Caribbean literature (*Littérature et identité créole aux Antilles*). Her latest books are *Infiltrating Culture: Power and Identity in Contemporary Women's Writing, Declining The Stereotype: Representation and Ethnicity in French Cultures,* and *Postcolonial Hospitality: the Immigrant as Guest.* She is currently studying the representation of "felicitous encounters" between France and the Maghreb.

FRANCESCA CANADÉ SAUTMAN is Executive Officer of the Ph.D. Program in French, The Graduate Center of CUNY. In addition to her work in the premodern era, she has published articles and essays on race, popular culture, and marginal communities in modern French and Francophone cultures. She is the author of *La religion du quotidien. Rites et croyances populaires de la fin du Moyen Age* (1995) and co-editor, with Pamela Sheingorn, of *Women and Same-Sex Desire in the Middle Ages* (2002).

RONNIE SCHARFMAN is Professor of French and Literature at Purchase College, SUNY. She is the author of numerous articles on Francophone writers. Her book on Aimé Césaire, *Engagement and the Language of the Subject in the Poetry of Aimé Césaire* (Florida, 1987), won a Gilbert Chinard Literary Prize. She co-edited a double volume of *Yale French Studies* on "Post/Colonial Conditions" with Françoise Lionnet (82–83, 1993), and an anthology of French and Francophone women writers, *Écritures de femmes* (Yale University Press, 1996) with Mary Ann Caws, Marianne Hirsch, and Mary Jean Green.

NAOMI SCHOR was Benjamin F. Barge Professor of French at Yale at the time of her death in December 2001. Her books included *Zola's Crowds, Breaking the Chain, Reading in Detail, George Sand and Idealism,* and *Bad Objects.* She was founding co-editor of *differences: a journal of feminist cultural studies.* In recent times she had embarked on a new project on French universalism that brought Francophone authors such as Senghor into her work.

JOSIAS SEMUJANGA taught at the National University of Rwanda and at the University of Western Ontario before becoming a professor at the University of Montréal, where he now teaches Francophone literature and literary theory. Among his published books: *Configuration de l'énonciation interculturelle dans le roman francophone* (1996); *Récits fondateurs du drame rwandais. Discours social, idéologies et stéréotypes* (1998); *Dynamique des genres dans le roman africain. Éléments de poétique transculturelle* (1999), and *The Origins of Rwandan Genocide* (2002).

ALYSON WATERS is Managing Editor of *Yale French Studies* and a translator. She teaches courses on translation and translation theory, and on bilingual writers, in the Yale French Department. Her translations include Louis Aragon's *Treatise on Style*, Tzvetan Todorov's *Morals of History*, and numerous articles and essays in the fields of art history and criticism. She was the guest editor of *Translation: The Translucent Art* (*Sites* 5/2, 2001). Her translation of Réda Bensmaïa's *Experimental Nations: The Invention of the Maghreb* is forthcoming from Princeton University Press.

The following issues are available through **Yale University Press,** Customer Service Department, P.O. Box 209040, New Haven, CT 06520-9040.

69 The Lesson of Paul de Man (1985) $17.00

73 Everyday Life (1987) $17.00

75 The Politics of Tradition: Placing Women in French Literature (1988) $17.00

Special Issue: After the Age of Suspicion: The French Novel Today (1989) $17.00

76 Autour de Racine: Studies in Intertextuality (1989) $17.00

77 Reading the Archive: On Texts and Institutions (1990) $17.00

78 On Bataille (1990) $17.00

79 Literature and the Ethical Question (1991) $17.00

Special Issue: Contexts: Style and Value in Medieval Art and Literature (1991) $17.00

80 Baroque Topographies: Literature/History/ Philosophy (1992) $17.00

81 On Leiris (1992) $17.00

82 Post/Colonial Conditions Vol. 1 (1993) $17.00

83 Post/Colonial Conditions Vol. 2 (1993) $17.00

84 Boundaries: Writing and Drawing (1993) $17.00

85 Discourses of Jewish Identity in 20th-Century France (1994) $17.00

86 Corps Mystique, Corps Sacré (1994) $17.00

87 Another Look, Another Woman (1995) $17.00

88 Depositions: Althusser, Balibar, Macherey (1995) $17.00

89 Drafts (1996) $17.00

90 Same Sex / Different Text? Gay and Lesbian Writing in French (1996) $17.00

91 Genet: In the Language of the Enemy (1997) $17.00

92 Exploring the Conversible World (1997) $17.00

93 The Place of Maurice Blanchot (1998) $17.00

94 Libertinage and Modernity (1999) $17.00

95 Rereading Allegory: Essays in Memory of Daniel Poirion (1999) $17.00

96 50 Years of *Yale French Studies,* Part I: 1948-1979 (1999) $17.00

97 50 Years of *Yale French Studies,* Part 2: 1980-1998 (2000) $17.00

98 The French Fifties (2000) $17.00

99 Jean-François Lyotard: Time and Judgment (2001) $17.00

100 FRANCE/USA: The Cultural Wars (2001) $17.00

101 Fragments of Revolution (2002) $17.00

102 Belgian Memories (2002) $17.00

Special subscription rates are available on a calendar-year basis (2 issues per year):
Individual subscriptions $26.00
Institutional subscriptions $30.00

ORDER FORM   Yale University Press, P.O. Box 209040, New Haven, CT 06520-9040
I would like to purchase the following individual issues:
_____
_____

For individual issues, please add postage and handling:
Single issue, United States $2.75   Each additional issue $.50
Single issue, foreign countries $5.00   Each additional issue $1.00
Connecticut residents please add sales tax of 6%.

Payment of $_____ is enclosed (including sales tax if applicable).

MasterCard no. _____ Expiration date _____

VISA no. _____ Expiration date _____

Signature _____

SHIP TO _____
_____
_____

See the next page for ordering other back issues. Yale French Studies is also available through Xerox University Microfilms, 300 North Zeeb Road, Ann Arbor, MI 48106.

The following issues are still available through the **Yale French Studies Office**, P.O. Box 208251, New Haven, CT 06520-8251.

19/20 Contemporary Art
$3.50

33 Shakespeare $3.50

35 Sade $3.50

39 Literature and Revolution
$3.50

42 Zola $5.00

43 The Child's Part $5.00

45 Language as Action $5.00

46 From Stage to Street $3.50

52 Graphesis $5.00

54 Mallarmé $5.00

61 Toward a Theory of
Description $6.00

Add for postage & handling

Single issue, United States $3.00 (Priority Mail)   Each additional issue $1.25
Single issue, United States $1.80 (Third Class)   Each additional issue $ .50
Single issue, foreign countries $2.50 (Book Rate)   Each additional issue $1.50

YALE FRENCH STUDIES, P.O. Box 208251, New Haven, Connecticut 06520-8251
A check made payable to YFS is enclosed. Please send me the following issue(s):

Issue no.   Title   Price

_____

_____

Postage & handling _____

Total _____

Name _____

Number/Street _____

City _____ State _____ Zip _____

- -

The following issues are now available through Periodicals Service Company, 11 Main Street, Germantown, N.Y. 12526, Phone: (518) 537-4700. Fax: (518) 537-5899.

1 Critical Bibliography of Existentialism
2 Modern Poets
3 Criticism & Creation
4 Literature & Ideas
5 The Modern Theatre
6 France and World Literature
7 André Gide
8 What's Novel in the Novel
9 Symbolism
10 French-American Literature Relationships
11 Eros, Variations...
12 God & the Writer
13 Romanticism Revisited
14 Motley: Today's French Theater
15 Social & Political France
16 Foray through Existentialism
17 The Art of the Cinema
18 Passion & the Intellect, or Malraux

19/20 Contemporary Art
21 Poetry Since the Liberation
22 French Education
23 Humor
24 Midnight Novelists
25 Albert Camus
26 The Myth of Napoleon
27 Women Writers
28 Rousseau
29 The New Dramatists
30 Sartre
31 Surrealism
32 Paris in Literature
33 Shakespeare in France
34 Proust
48 French Freud
51 Approaches to Medieval Romance

36/37 Structuralism has been reprinted by Doubleday as an Anchor Book.
55/56 Literature and Psychoanalysis has been reprinted by Johns Hopkins University Press, and can
    be ordered through Customer Service, Johns Hopkins University Press, Baltimore, MD 21218.